D1598940

the

DICTIONARY

of

HINDUSTANI

CLASSICAL

MUSIC

the

DICTIONARY

of

HINDUSTANI

CLASSICAL

MUSIC

Pandit Amarnath

Foreword by REKHA BHARDWAJ

PENGUIN BOOKS

An imprint of Penguin Random House

VIKING

USA | Canada | UK | Ireland | Australia
New Zealand | India | South Africa | China

Viking is part of the Penguin Random House group of companies
whose addresses can be found at global.penguinrandomhouse.com

Published by Penguin Random House India Pvt. Ltd
7th Floor, Infinity Tower C, DLF Cyber City,
Gurgaon 122 002, Haryana, India

First published in Viking by Penguin Random House India 2020

10 9 8 7 6 5 4 3 2 1

The views and opinions expressed in this book are the author's own and the
facts are as reported by him which have been verified to the extent possible,
and the publishers are not in any way liable for the same.

ISBN 9780670092277

Typeset in Adobe Garamond Pro by Manipal Technologies Limited, Manipal
Printed at Replika Press Pvt. Ltd, India

www.penguin.co.in

To Smt. Jaidevi, my late mother,
whose dim memories I have lived by

Foreword

Rekha Bhardwaj

Guru bin gyaan na paae,
mann moorakh soch soch kaahe pachhtae,
Satguru ki sangat kar re,
Re gyaani, tab guniyan mein guni kahaay

(There is no knowledge without a guru,
Foolish heart, why waste time on your illusions,
Spend time under the feet of a spiritual master
Only then will you be deemed erudite amongst the
knowledgeable)

A tall man dressed in comfortably fitted trousers and a tweed coat, muffler around his neck like vines encircling the strong trunk, front lock of hair resting on his forehead, Guru-ji, with his magnificent stature, was like a big banyan tree—under the shadow of this tree we disciples rested, relaxed, gained strength and learnt humility.

He walked with poise—steady and grounded, reaching the heights in his own being, inspiring us. When I walked alongside

Guru-ji, I always felt proud and safe, mesmerized by his sage-like persona. I was a young girl back then, barely eighteen, while he must have been fifty-seven! Those walks were more like a discourse, sometimes in silence, at other times, words of wisdom seeping into my subconscious, subtly adding to my personality without me being aware of it. A man of few words, he could silently inspire you to take courage in your hands. His perceptive eye could read you inside-out, you could hide nothing from him.

The first image etched in my mind and heart is watching Guru-ji perform in Aiwan-e-Ghalib Auditorium, sitting with both palms resting on the floor, singing—sometimes with his eyes closed—like a dhyaani (meditator), at other times eyes open, looking at the audience. When he sang something intricate, the spark in his eyes lit up the auditorium. I was only eight years old then. The second time I saw him, I was seventeen years old, taking part in an All-India Music Competition. Here, I witnessed an unbiased and impartial guru who favoured the best performances over those of his own students.

After almost a year, I went to seek admission in his class at Bharatiya Kala Kendra. He would always hold an audition before accepting a student and he would only take disciples who were trained in basics. Though he had heard me sing a ghazal, he asked me if I could sing the taan (combination of notes in a particular scale sung in a fast tempo) that had just been sung in Raga Alhaiya Bilawal in the class. I said I could try, and I did sing the same. I saw him glance at all of his students with the same spark that I had seen when I had seen him perform.

I was destined to meet Guru-ji and learn from him in this life . . . These relationships are predestined. I strongly believe in cosmic connections. I always feel that music is ibaadat to me. and reading this very quote later in his book *Conversations with Pandit Amarnath* revealed why I felt this unspoken bond and deep connect with Guru-ji despite being naïve and not wise at all at that point of time. Sometimes he would chuckle and say, '*Bechari Rekha, sari duniya ka bhaar iske kandhon par hai.*' (Poor Rekha, she carries the burden of the entire world on her shoulders.) He never discouraged me from pouring my heart out.

Reading the short biography of Guru-ji included in this book, I learnt so much about his childhood, his lonesome life and Sufi-connect, how he coped with his pain and his longing. If I trace back my history with Guru-ji, my relationship actually started as a baby as I used to listen to two of his 'Sufiana Kalaams' with Pandit Vinod Mudgal that were broadcast on All India Radio in the programme *Vandana* at 6 in the morning: '*Main Nirguniya Gun Nahi Mo Mein*' and '*Tu Saancha Sahib Mera*'. These had an eternal impact on the artiste and being in me. I may have been singing 'Sufi Kalaam' since 2002 but then the seed was sown when I was just a kid, and Guru-ji has to be credited for it.

'Riyaaz today is taken as a practice or exercise. The difference is of the spirit. If done with a spirit of devotion, the exercise becomes riyaazat, ibaadat,' he would often say. He always said that the most important riyaaz is to listen to yourself while you sing . . . I follow this to date. Guru-ji was a musicians' musician. He was a poet at heart, musicologist, author and a great guru. He equipped us with tools to explore and create all kinds of permutations and combinations to discover our strengths and weaknesses. He did not want us to be dependent on him but become independent thinkers and innovators, and carve our own path.

Initially, he would teach us individually for fifteen minutes each, for the rest of the time we were allowed to sit in class and listen to others. During those fifteen minutes we received material enough to work on (riyaz) for a lifetime. I still haven't been able to explore all of it . . . it is like a deep sea . . . the more you dive in, the deeper it gets.

When he sang in class his voice sounded extremely sweet as if coated with honey, so different from when he sang on mic which was more like a baritone, a *manjhi hui, sadhhi hui awaaz.*

I would call him an evolved modern guru with strong values, at the same time demanding discipline and sadhana. He was a giver, never asked us to hide anything from anyone, he always believed in sharing. He believed firmly in the guru–shishya parampara and maintained those values even in the changed ambience of a private fine arts institute where we learnt. He was a human being of great class, ethics, principles, compassion and understanding and so very accepting. He was full of pride and self-respect, at the same time, a simple man who enjoyed watching Amitabh Bachchan movies.

The content of this book is inspired by his students' queries on various aspects of music, its complexities as well as the personal struggles Guru-ji faced during lessons and riyaz.

Pinjar surmandal bhayaa,
Surat surat ka mela,
Chintan dwaare an milo re,
Saat suran kee belaa.

(The harp is the cage of life bound by its ribs
Where word meets melody
And opens the door of consciousness.
O come meet me at sense's door for my spirit
calls with its seven notes)

This came about when a Dutch student asked him about Shrutees. 'Why twenty-two?' He checked that there were twenty-two ribs in the ribcage and was struck by the oneness of body structure, breath and sound, and came to compose the above-mentioned song.

He felt concerned that *sohbat*, an essential part of training under the guru–shishya parampara, was becoming rare. One day, Guru-ji and I were walking from Bharatiya Kala Kendra to the Shriram Centre bus stop. Suddenly, after we reached the end of Bahawalpur House to cross the road, he stopped me, saying, 'Beta, I want to say something to you'. He continued, 'It is rare that a shishya meets the guru at the right time and the guru meets the right shishya at the correct time. It has happened, so make the most of it. Do your riyaz regularly.'

I still carry in my subconscious mind the responsibility he thus placed on me. When I met Shantanu Ray Chaudhuri at a literary fest, during dinner I asked him if it was possible to publish this book since I wished to share this gift of my Guru-ji with fellow artistes, upcoming musicians, students and lovers of music. Shantanu asked for the manuscript and upon reading it, immediately agreed, asking me to write the foreword and also provide updates. After discussions with Gajra, my guru-behen (Guru-ji's younger daughter), we decided to add profiles of a few contemporary artistes whom he had purposely not included when he published the book in 1989. That is my little contribution to this edition. My apologies if a few names have been left out inadvertently. The omission is totally unintentional.

This book also gives a peek into the culture of idioms, proverbs, *muhavre* that were used regularly in artistic vocabulary. One term that I love is *chinakdaaree*—*chinak* means drizzle, also a sweet pinpricking, refers to music charged throughout with bristling (spark-like) creativity.

To quote Guru-ji himself: 'The great wealth of terminology and proverbial expression in Hindustani music represents, symbolically, much of its content, and for musicians, their shishyas, and lovers of music, the arrows and landmarks of a long inward journey . . . This collection brings together more than 600 terms (words, phrases, proverbs and sayings, presented here in alphabetical order) from the Hindustani music tradition, unfolding this great art as karma yoga, gyana yoga as well as bhakti yoga . . . After forty-five years of performing, writing, composing, research and teaching, I have felt the need to record my experiences in the shape of this "language" of Hindustani music, the language and taste of living in music.'

He said, 'The time indeed will come when it shall become an essential experience for every member of the Hindustani music world.' That time has come . . . this book is being published at the right time . . . it is the need of today. I would especially recommend this book for schools, colleges and universities to keep in libraries while all students should have it in their personal collection.

I cannot count my blessings and thank my stars enough for being with Guru-ji as it brought very precious people into my life. Amarjeet didi, Guru-ji's senior-most disciple with whom I continue to learn with complete trust ever since Guru-ji left for his heavenly abode. Shanti Vaidyanathan Sharma fondly called 'Shanti-di' who had us awestruck with her grasp over her craft each time she had a lesson with Guru-ji. Bindo-di as we called Bindu Chawla, Guru-ji's elder daughter who treated us like her own, giving us a wealth of Guru-ji's books. Her foundation also released a few of Guru-ji's CDs. The biography that she was writing before her sudden demise in 2017 is being published in this book after further editing by Gajra; Nisha Mahajan, my guru-behen, Kathak exponent and founder of Tyaag (The Yoga And Art Group), my spiritual mentor, confidante, and to date, my pillar of strength.

Since Guru-ji kept himself in tune with the youth, he chose English as the medium for the book, realizing that the book would probably reach more people that way. It gives me great pleasure to share this rare gift that Guru-ji gave us, apart from the unparalleled treasure of more than 200 bandishes of his own under the pen-name 'Miturang' that he bequeathed to the Indore gharaanaa. I, along with Gajra, plan to bring out more books and music of Guru-ji to share with the world. *The Dictionary of Hindustani Classical Music* is a must-have for all music lovers.

Introduction to the Original Edition

Arrows and landmarks on the roadside make the traveller's journey towards his destination easier. The great wealth of terminology and proverbial expression in Hindustani music represents, symbolically, much of its content, and for musicians, their shishyas, and lovers of music, the arrows and landmarks of a long inward journey.

This collection brings together more than 600 terms (words, phrases, proverbs and sayings, presented here in alphabetical order) from the Hindustani music tradition, unfolding this great art as karma yoga, gyana yoga as well as bhakti yoga. In other words gyana (or knowledge), which is meaningless without karma (or doing), karma which is blind without gyana, and both being complete only with bhakti (or devotion and faith). After forty-five years of performing, writing, composing, research and teaching, I have felt the need to record my experiences in the shape of this 'language' of Hindustani music, the language and taste of living in music.

The vocabulary collected here was still in use till about my early musical age—the early 1940s—before music spread into the universities. However, much of it has now fallen into disuse with the dying out of the gharaanaa (or traditional school) environment.

For as young shishyas we not only lived at the feet of our gurus but, what has really become rare today, we had the opportunity to listen to the great masters in conversation with each other, informally talking for hours about musicians and music. It was in this manner that we imbibed ideas about the attitudes as well as techniques of the masters as we saw them living through entire musical processes. Thus, a special feature of this dictionary is the inclusion of the sayings of the masters, almost like proverbs for us today.

Through the process of working on this book, I also recalled many crucial questions, which my own shishyas put to me from time to time. An otherwise brilliant student would usually falter at the taan portion of her singing; she would often sing half-heartedly at this point, though obviously through no real incapability. 'Guru-ji, why is there no rasa or bhaava in the taan, whereas when I do aalaap it is full of emotion and endless expression?' I answered by first giving her some clues as to how taans were taught by the old masters: by identifying them with names to suit their designing and structuring. This is known as dhobee-pataraa, this utthaa-patak, this guththam-gutthaa; this is sapaat and this choot. What could all these signify? What emotion or bhaava but the sheer sense of thrill communicated through their structural variations and accents when rendered skilfully? The sign of relief was obvious on my student's face. Some of this phraseology I would then add into this volume.

Through the years I also came across some students with keen, questioning minds who demanded, along with their regular lessons, a body of language with which they could write on the subject. So for them I analysed extensively. Musicians and teachers earlier were generally not in the habit of doing this. It was not needed either, for their method of learning and teaching in any case covered most of these things. This is how, in fact, the present volume took shape. And it was written in English because I was using this language, if not always, at least part of the time to communicate to students from a wide cross-section of regions in India.

The problems that students identified were most inspiring at times. A Dutch student once asked a challenging question about shrutees. What persuaded the Hindu mind to arrive at a fixation of shrutees at twenty-two? I postponed the clarification to the next sitting, as I wanted to explore the question myself. That evening I asked my son, then a medical student, how many ribs we had in the lungs. Eleven pairs, he replied, one on each side and two accessories—non-functional in the sound-producing system. I was struck by the oneness of body structure, breath and sound and came to compose this song:

> *Pinjar surmandal bhayaa,*
> *Surat surat ka mela,*
> *Chintan dwaare an milo re,*
> *Saat suran kee belaa.*

> (The harp is the cage of life bound by its ribs
> Where word meets melody
> And opens the door of consciousness.
> O come meet me at sense's door for my spirit calls
> with its seven notes)

It is thus that compositions are born and perhaps also how musical proverbs emerge out of the insights of the masters, reflected in their daily observations. For, much of the terminology here can be traced in its origin to the perceptions and understanding of the masters.

Explored thus in terms of musical practice, the words express a music that is sung as well as felt and taught—and in this fashion the present collection could be said to differ from a purely musicological work. For, in the theoretical area this volume emphasizes only on those concepts and terminology that can be understood meaningfully in terms of music that is actually practised today. Students, and musicians as well, are often confused as to the differences between the grammatical terminology that was in use during the past (and by past I would mean from about the thirteenth century onwards), and that which is in use today.[1]

Those associated with syllabi-oriented teaching and learning are often sadly bogged down by theoretical concepts that have long been dissociated from the practice of classical music. This volume, in its selection of terms and their interpretations, hopes to restore to students, musicians as well as listeners, the necessary sense of clarity in terms of the grammar of music, as well as balance in the sifting of myth from historical fact.

Tansen's Menu

I would like to point out that there is very little in this text of history and purely historical references. I have always felt that at least Indian music history, in the shape in which it is available to us today, is not essential to the understanding of the fundamentals of music. The number of hours Tansen practised, his breakfast menu after riyaz, or the number of his wives—these are not the musicians' concerns.

As I have pointed out already, the terms and proverbs contained herein will help ascertain the minds of musicians of the past—but not their history. On the other hand, the study of musical periods (Vedic period to the present day, about which some data is

---

[1]　See for example, the explanations on *Saptak* and *Ashtak* in the appendix titled 'Some Points of Controversy in Hindustani Music'.

available), which is also referred to as history, amounts to external evidence of Hindustani music alone. Those directly concerned with Indian music in the past did not record history in a deeper sense, as we had no notation system. True internal evidence of our past, by which I mean the possibility of reimagining the styles and structures of classical music of the past through materials available at present, is a subject of musical 'anthropology', to put it in today's language. This is not an easy area, and it can be a truly rewarding experience to the most visionary of musicians alone. Unfortunately, we have at times allowed ourselves to be weighed down by a sense of the largeness and greatness of the past, taking recourse to such historical examples and references.

As mentioned already, I have, from the very beginning, written this dictionary in English because of its utility, of being able to communicate to the largest possible number of readers. I feel that there are definitely more readers in English than those in Hindi and these include concert audiences as well as academicians (linguists, ethnomusicologists and so on), students as well as young musicians. Even within my country I have had to use English—or partly English—to talk to a person from, say, the south or Bengal.

It is a great task for an Indian musician to explain Hindustani terms in English, especially avoiding conditioned explanations and comparisons of Hindustani terms with those from Western music terminology. For instance, I have not made use of words like 'glissando' in explaining meend, 'interval' for distances between notes within the scale, 'mode' in the explanation of raga, 'tremolo' for gamak, or 'microtone' for shrutee. I feel that too free a borrowing of these terms brings in the inevitable element of comparison. A comparison of fine musical details of two disparate civilizations and cultures. This is the danger zone where errors can arise.

To take an example, gamak is a deliberate movement between two specific notes, whereas tremolo, which is often used to explain gamak, refers to a tonal variety of sound (on one note), sound which contains a sense of tremulousness. Gamak is not trembling on a note. If we compare the movements by taking the example of a ball, tremolo would be the bouncing of the sound ball on the floor and gamak the hitting of the sound ball from wall to wall. Besides, through such comparisons of Indian terms with Western music, the charm of fresh, unconditioned understanding is lost on the listener as well. Therefore, I have tried to work out a body of language that has grown out of the process of handling the materials of Hindustani music itself.

At the same time terms like 'voice culture', 'tone' and 'pitch' have been included in the present collection. The terms have certainly been easily absorbed into present-day vocabulary in Hindustani music. They were technically required in the era of recording systems. Besides, there are no terms in the Hindustani language that could communicate these concepts—or if there are, their equivalents in Hindustani are generally not heard. For while tone refers to the character of sound, pitch is to set the key, voice-culture is the maximum possible cultivation of vocalization and the culturing of tone.

While on the subject of usage of terms, we find many terms that are used quite vaguely while talking of music. Shrutee in Carnatic music is used for any swara or semitone, as well as for even stating a pitch. Gamak is used in Carnatic music for any small, shaking piece of music, taan for any small or big piece. Khatkaa, murkee and phandaa in Hindustani music are used for any small ornamental twist, or thrilling piece; jagah for any special piece in music. So, readers will find that there are many expressions used for one thing in music, and for one expression so many words tend to be used.

And now we come to the entries on the musicians themselves. I have included only the late masters—especially those of the early twentieth century, whom I had the privilege of hearing. But I have left out contemporary musicians—all those that are living today—to avoid chronicling one's own times, the delicacies of writing about one's contemporaries. Besides, unlike the musicians of today, very little has been written about musicians of the past. Readers will find the entries on musicians listed on the basis of first names, not surnames. This is because they have, by and large, been known that way.[2]

I have also left out ragas from this collection altogether, because there is enough good literature available in this area. There are, among others, the six-volume *Kramik Pustakmaalika* by Bhatkhande and the seven-volume *Raag Vigyaan* by V.N. Patwardhan—both authoritative works on the subject. And then, by listing ragas I will not be able to help the readers much—for Hindustani music is an oral tradition that ultimately has to be transferred from master to pupil literally. For, in the unique system of the basic and original Hindustani ragas it is not just about the layout of the notes or the dimensional accuracy of the planning of the two halves (uttaraang-poorvaang). It is also about the accent of each note in each raga which is the real secret of rendering the raga.

For example, the Komal Rishab of Bhairav will not be used in Jogia or in Gunkalee as it is used in Bhairav, though the note is the same. Similarly, the Dhaivat of Bhopaalee and Deshkaar is the same but used differently. In Bhopaalee, it is in an up-to-down movement, indicating night, and in Deshkar, it has a lower to high emphasis, depicting dawn. Again, Maarwaah and Puriyaa

---

[2] Editor's note: Rekha Bhardwaj has updated the names by including some contemporary musicians.

have the same notes but their Rishab keeps the distinction. There are countless groups of ragas from the same thaaths but they are different at every step, accent-wise and emphasis-wise. On every note you have to keep the marked distinction throughout the rendering (in the faster or more thrilling portions, this emphasis or accent of individual notes becomes a bit relaxed).

Hindustani ragas have never lent themselves to notation either. Performing a raga is like painting a portrait; every time you sing the same raga, you paint an original portrait and not a copy. The truly great performance is never pre-composed, it is the on-the-spot expression of your overall creative capacity. Thus this dictionary—as indeed any other work on Hindustani music—must be read absolutely in the context of such a non-static tradition.

Though written in a dictionary format, I think this volume could be read from cover to cover. It will be of relevance to the linguistic researcher too. Many words here belong to the category of spoken dialect, and have been explained in a relative sense, as a result. There are Persian, Urdu and Sanskrit usages, as also everyday speech forms of the common folk. Because of the latter, sometimes words have been used approximately rather than literally by the musicians themselves. These have a charm of their own, indicating a live experience of music. As such they provide a true glimpse of the inner life of the art and of musicians in India.

Amarnath

A Daughter Remembers

Bindu Chawla

It is strange the kind of memories that overwhelm you when you start to think back about your parents, particularly one who has been so accomplished, practically a genius. For example, for some reason the first thought that strikes me is the way he signed his name 'Amarnath' in Hindi—without the matra on top. Also, he never liked to use his last name, Chawla (which meant the owner of wells; harking to his familial occupation of being zamindars). So he preferred just Amarnath, another name of Lord Shiva. 'Nath' was a silent yet lifelong identification with the wandering minstrels and bards of the north, that is, with the Nath yogi parampara.

He was proud to be born on the cusp, 22 March, when there appeared tender new leaves on trees big and small and on trees young and old. The sense of new life, the innocence of it. Similar was his love for the best part of the day—early dawn, or 'bhor', as he used to say; the tender new day. Internally, that was the perennial state of mind he was in; a state of new leaves and tender innocence all through the seven decades that life granted him. True spirituality, he would claim, is the 'unconditioned decisions of your mind', untouched by motives and reasons.

As a child, he would often spend the early hours of the morning (prabhat) gazing out of his window, fascinated by the occasional wandering jogi and the fakeer, watching them pass by, as if through the pages of a Dickensian novel. They would be humming a ditty about life, an intense one-on-one with God, barely there with the world and living with utmost simplicity. And it was this simplicity that was the hallmark of Pandit-ji's life. When all the people were wearing embroidered shawls with carvings on their instruments, he felt bad because *ibadat* called for no ostentation when it came to relating to God; the musician should give in to fakeeri, he believed. All saints aspire for austerity because that is the road to *barkat*. He believed that it was only then that the heart would overflow and God would give the person what he wants. It is then that God asks his devotee, *'Bol teri raza kya hai?'* That is His nature.

As he narrated many times, Pandit-ji's first taste of musical sound had a rather painful story behind it. Pandit-ji's earliest memories were those of his mother in bed with tuberculosis. They were not poor, but Pandit-ji said that his mother had a habit of caring for her husband and her son to the point of neglecting herself completely. Consequently, she wilted young. Those days tuberculosis was considered highly contagious and necessary precautions were taken to isolate the patient. She was shifted to the verandah of the house, on to a huge charpai, or a four-poster bed woven in strong jute, with a sand-filled thook-dan or spitting-bowl by her side. The charpai was placed at an angle from which she would take sad and helpless glances at her son playing close by. Jaidevi was her name, but Pandit-ji took her name only a few times in his life, like you would the name of the Lord, but cried out for her at certain hard-to-bear moments of his life when he would simply utter *'O meri Ma!'*

Then came the day when she was taken away. Ma was gone. The charpai was now empty. Despite living with her impending death for four years, accepting the reality was hard. He was inconsolable. Before he knew it, he had climbed on to the charpai and was crying desperately. Gradually, as he was still sobbing, without really knowing why, he started to pluck at the square weaves of the manji, the jute strings of the charpai still so full of Ma, and began to feel a strange consolation. He then plucked more consciously, and felt a strong thrill down his spine, the sound was more than full of appeal . . . and thus came the moment that would be etched in his memory forever.

Music, it seems, was in his blood. He had heard that when his Ma was in good health, she used to sing folk songs and was especially sought after during weddings and other family rituals like the birth of children. It's possible that she had far-off family links with the dholas and dholnis or professional folk musicians of Jhang known collectively as Jhang ke dhole—for Jhang was full of them.

Close to Jhang, in Lyallpur, Pandit-ji found comfort in his maternal grandfather, his Nana-ji who was known to be a noble soul who kept a *sadabrat* or fast, which he observed all his life. He would feed the poor once a week every week of his life, for as long as he lived. He opened the door of his house to anybody who would come in on that one day of the week and feed them a meal with his own hands, handing out water and a towel for washing hands at the end of it all. He never discriminated and was generous to a fault.

Pandit-ji's Nana-ji would often go off to Jhang to fetch his little 'Nath', as they used to call him, to 'be with him for a few days' and was almost all the time in a state of anxiety about him, especially after his daughter's illness. Ma had been his only child, who too had lost her mother when she was little. Naturally, Nana-ji spoilt him. Nath would ride on his Nana-ji's shoulders through the market town of Lyallpur, and was cuddled warm into Nana-ji's razai, the heaviest quilt you could think of, long before the cold set in during early winter evenings.

Though Nana-ji never worked, he owned property, around four to five houses and one shop, the power of attorney of which was given to Pandit-ji at the time of Nana-ji's demise. Pandit-ji was only eight years old at that time.

Pandit-ji's Dada-ji (paternal grandfather) also held a special place in the memories of his grandson. His name was Devi Dayal, known as Lala Devi Dayal—Chawla affixed sometimes—in those parts, a tall and handsome man with a king-sized turban which he wore old style, fanning small on top of the head on the right and long over the shoulder; he walked with an umbrella to match. After the British rule, men in undivided India had turned to wearing coats over their dhoti-kurta, and so, with his height, Dada-ji looked near aristocratic in his simple white dress.

Dada-ji had another interesting trait. Though he was not exactly a miser, he was known to chew a single-anna coin a little at the side before starting the next round of family expenditure. It was believed that you are thrifty with money if you did that. Pandit-ji went back to these memories and shared them with his children often, never being judgemental and remaining full of the wonder of childhood, of little boys starstruck at their grandfathers.

Pandit-ji often spoke about his Dada-ji who was known to be such an evolved soul that he actually predicted the day and hour of his demise. So, on the day of the passing he took an early morning bath, asked all the women folk of the house to come out of the kitchen and be bathed and dressed as well, for he wanted to save them negative associations with what was to follow. He then asked his son to sit on the floor and hold his head on his lap, till he took the last breath . . . for it was thought to be most auspicious if you died on the lap of your son. And as the extended family gathered around his body, wailing and weeping, he asked for the oil-wick or diya also to be lit.

* * *

Pandit-ji, who lived with his father and stepmother, had, at a rather tender age, become much sought-after for singing chaupais or verses from the Ramayana at the satsangs at the town's holy temple. In fact, Swami Gurcharan Das-ji, who was said to be his stepmother's guru-ji and was the mahant or priest of the only temple in Jhang, became so fond of the little boy and his emotional renderings of the epic that he would often say he wanted to take Pandit-ji along with him to lead the life of a priest and adopting him as his spiritual son.

These early sanskars or influences are immensely important in the life of any true artist and his renderings were all the more poignant and charged for the helplessness and torture he went through in his daily life. They gave him an alternative he could believe in, a confirmation of the beauty and goodness of life. These renderings from the Ramayana would bring tears to the eyes of the old women who sat in the front rows of the satsang and ironically bring a lot of attention to his stepmother. The next day these women would whisper to each other at the market, when they saw her, that 'Nath' was her 'chhora' or lad. With that little shot of fame, his mother's immense bitterness for the stepson would fade for a while and she would loudly declare at dinner that Nath be served an extra spoonful of ghee in his katori of daal or bowl of lentils.

His stepmother, the first cousin of his biological mother, was only fifteen-and-a-half years old at the time she married Pita-ji. He was, at the time, twenty-seven. Her age was no bar on the kind of influence she would wield on him throughout their lives. When

Pandit-ji was little, his maternal family had asked to keep him, but Pita-ji would not hear of it. As a result, not a single day passed when Pandit-ji slept on a dry pillow. The emotional ostracism was constant and went on for as long as he lived in his father's house and abated somewhat only when he was able to earn a living and move away. Sometimes his eyes streamed for hours in the silence of the night; perhaps that is why he acquired a permanent look of sadness, even a tinge of horror.

He never picked on memories of his stepmother, but this one, like many others, never faded from his memory. One afternoon, she repeatedly asked him, 'When your father comes home in the evening, tell him you want another mother, say it.' In the innocence of childhood, he said, '*Pita-ji, Pita-ji, mainu nai maa laa deyo.*' Pita-ji slapped him so hard that the horror and shock were etched on his heart forever. To an uncomprehending child, the world was like an enemy. A world which hurt all the time. And so, the Lord became his all-time lover, the only balm for his constantly traumatized soul. '*Yahi ghar soona, ut mangal baaje; it piya roothe, ut hans gal laage; aisi nagariya anoop, utth to chale re avadhoot.*' 'This home is a lonely one, but there it is all auspiciousness; here my love is gravely annoyed, but there He laughs and envelops me in embrace, O, such is that unique world . . . the Avadhoot, the pious man, has arisen from this world.'

Once Pandit-ji's father remarried, each year a sibling was born. He was no longer the focus of Pita-ji's world. As often happens, the proceeds of the property left by Nana-ji that were rightfully Pandit-ji's were used up by Pita-ji in bringing up his brood of children born after Pandit-ji. There used to be endless family debates about what happened to all that property, why it was not handed over to Pandit-ji when he turned eighteen, or how it was sold and where all the money went. Pandit-ji never asked his Pita-ji about the property, but perhaps did yearn for some acknowledgement about how the proceeds did help tide over the difficult years. No such word came, however, and instead, Pandit-ji was removed from school, even though he did very well in class, standing first in two of the five subjects he studied—his all-time favourites, geography and history. The reason Pandit-ji was given for his education being discontinued was an apparent lack of finances.

However, in lieu of the education, and seeing his love for music, Pita-ji brought home a harmonium for his music-loving son as compensation. Even this was highly grudged at home, as they all felt that Pita-ji had 'indulged' his first-born. It was expensive, by the standards of the day, but somehow Pita-ji felt very happy to gift this to him. It soon became an extension of Pandit-ji's personality. It also came to mark the earliest period of his tryst with music, in which he was mainly self-taught, another sign of the prodigy that he actually was.

It wasn't just education that Pandit-ji had to sacrifice. Much later, his stepmother also objected to his alliance with a well-known musician of the Kirana gharaanaa on grounds that the girl's family was upper class, and they would not be able to cope with that. Giving in, Pandit-ji still held an abiding love for her as she did for him. Many people confirmed that whenever she would hear Pandit-ji sing, she would break down.

All said and done, his childhood was a difficult one and he was always tortured when it came to the concept of motherhood—especially as his father brought him up without any stories and memories that mentioned his mother. He longed for memories of her, what she looked like, what she liked to eat, to wear . . . But Pita-ji's silence was like a silent betrayal, a deep wound on his soul which never healed. But there was one memory—a single one that Pita-ji gave him, and which he held on to for dear life. A worn-out black Kashmiri woolen rug with white flowers embroidered on it, on which she had lain for a long, long time. 'Here, take this,' Pita-ji had said, 'it belongs to your mother.' Pandit-ji had brought the rug with him to India after Partition, along with his only prized possession, his taanpura.

Perhaps this is why he loved the colour black. He chose it as the colour of the flooring of the house he built in Delhi's artists' colony across the Yamuna. It was unconventional, but he stood his ground, and never really explained why. Otherwise, a faddist for white, handsome as he was, he was known widely in music circles for the pure-white shirt and trousers that almost became his signature style, especially during the years he was with All India Radio (AIR). Even after that, there was the pure-white kurta and pyjama he wore at the Triveni Kala Sangam, where he taught for almost eighteen years, the white muting to an off-white or such shades as the years wore on, his favourite being chai ka rang, or the colour of tea, he used to say. In deeper shades, however, it was coffee (which he adorably spelt as 'see-o-fee-fee ').

When he travelled, however, Pandit-ji lived up to the proverb, while in Rome, live as the Romans do. So, he sometimes even invented dress styles. Once in Italy, they recommended that he wear a jacket made from a material called 'pile', said to be the warmest cloth in the world, and he did. When he brought the cloth, he asked the theatre tailor to sew it for him—he was a guest of the Teatro Tascabile de Bergamo, who followed the Grotowski school of acting, and being their guest, he had been touring and performing all over Italy.

* * *

Pandit-ji's relatives were constantly concerned when it came to him, and so, there was always a check on the 'new mother'. There was his Bua, Pita-ji's widowed sister, a lady of humble means, who loved him dearly, but did not have the means to take him under her wing to bring him up.

Bua-ji loved Pandit-ji's children just as much. She was fond of bringing 'kheel' or the square-shaped pieces of puffed rice gelled with jaggery, which Pandit-ji loved to eat. The telephone was not such a common thing those days, so she would arrive unannounced at Pandit-ji's house and sometimes come just to reassure herself as he left the house to report to the radio station at noon.

* * *

Back in Pandit-ji's childhood days, the freedom movement had reached its crescendo and in a flush of patriotic emotion, Pita-ji gave up his high-powered job at the railways, and brought home a charkha. He would spin all day, and in the evening he would sell the chaadar he had woven at Jhang's little market, and bring home vegetables and other home essentials with the money earned.

In fact, with the freedom movement, the lifestyle of the entire family changed. Gone was Pita-ji's promise of building Pandit-ji a public library on a large piece of land they owned in Chowk Bazar, Jhang, where he would live a life of leisure. Pita-ji had originally dreamed this for him because despite his lack of education, Pandit-ji had a literary bent of mind. He had a voracious appetite for books and read all the time, both in English and in Hindi. A lot in Urdu too, for it was a popular language in those parts at that time, and he developed such a love for Urdu that he spoke to his family his entire life in a Hindustanized Urdu.

Despite all his constraints, Pita-ji never wanted Amarnath—his eldest son—to take up a career; he wanted him to remain a dreamer. 'Kaka,' he would say lovingly, 'I want you to read, write, sing and be a free man . . .'

So, a dreamer he remained, with one foot steeped in reality, keeping up with the regulations at home—though Mata-ji kept a spick-and-span kitchen, one where you could virtually see your face in the gleaming thalis in which they ate. Simple boiled potatoes were the order of the day. They were kept especially for him, for he ate at odd hours due to long hours of riyaz—but he never complained. Eventually, he took to eating some of the street food of those times. He was an ardent fan of the kachaloo, which was spiced so strongly that he had to blow his nose out after having them. Nothing could tear him away from the daily afternoon call of the kachaloo-wala, ringing his little bells as he rode the lanes of their house in Jhang.

Among the other flavours of childhood he remembered were the vegetables that came from the khoos, especially the kaalkaan, a variety of the gourd family, which was roasted in the embers of the chulha as the rotis were cooked, and then peeled, mashed and sprinkled with salt and pepper before being eaten. Later in his life, Pandit-ji would always insist the kaalkaan not be cut and pressure-cooked, but roasted over the gas burner, in an attempt to recapture the flavour of his childhood.

During winters, he would go for long early morning walks with his friends, all of them wearing 'chesters' or full-sleeved leather jackets. Those were the days of the Raj, the last leg of the Raj though, a pre-Partition culture where even films from Hollywood were a routine part of city life. Clark Gable and Greta Garbo were the hot favourites. Those winter mornings were severely cold for sure, and to keep warm, they would eat boiled eggs during these walks. Nobody was to mention this in front of Mata-ji, however, because she would undoubtedly lose her temper if she heard of this.

Just as there was extreme cold in Jhang as much as in Lahore—where they sometimes stayed, since Pita-ji worked in the

Indian Railways—there were extreme summers as well. Glorious summers marked by sandstorms that swept the towns and cities. They started in the evenings and sometimes continued the entire night, even sweeping away the outer walls of the city. These tall walls were known as kadhaliyan (the word came from the word kadh, or height), protective walls around the ramparts of the city. The sandstorms had a metaphysical relationship with the life of the people and that is why Pandit-ji always spoke all the more affectionately about the kadhaliyan. As little children, they were told to stay within the cosy, defining limits of these walls and never venture into the unknowingness of what lay beyond, the desert itself.

* * *

In 1942, at the age of eighteen, Pandit-ji gave his first performance at Lahore Radio. In the same year, a few months later, he began taking lessons from his first guru, Prof. B.N. Datta-ji, in Lahore itself. This first broadcast made a hero out of him, because the moment he stepped out of the radio station, scores of college students encircled him, actually picking him up and transporting him to the city's coffee house for a celebration. It was not a small thing, this broadcast, for it was from the Lahore station of AIR, and he became the youngest musician on the rolls of a galaxy of veterans.

Pandit-ji spent five years in apprenticeship with Datta-ji, a remarkable human being. He was kindness incarnate, gentle, graceful and dignified. Having lost his father when he was just a little boy, with seven sisters to take care of, Datta-ji's day started at the crack of dawn, and he took tuitions from morning till night. He taught and taught and taught all day, and started his own riyaz late in the night, only once all his students had left. It was at that time Pandit-ji bonded with him, sometimes playing the taanpura as he sang and sometimes giving theka, that is, accompanying him on the tabla. One of the things Pandit-ji often recounted was that even the ivory keys of the harmonium Datta-ji used when he taught his students had caved in, or as he said, '*un mein tak gaddhe par gaye thay*'. This was the stuff of which the musicians of that time were made of.

Datta-ji and Pandit-ji were constantly fighting for the other's well-being. 'Eat this regularly, and look after your health, or else . . .', 'Please take a little breather between one student and the next, why are you subjecting yourself to the daily grind in this fashion?' To the extent that one day, that one singular day in five years when Pandit-ji had some commitment at home and had not turned up at Datta-ji's, the latter actually went over to find out why. He stood in the middle of the lane of Pandit-ji's house in Lahore and, looking up at the first-floor windows to his house, shouted, 'Amarnath, come downstairs, what are you doing up there today?'

Those days Datta-ji was not yet married; he married at the age of forty in Delhi after the Partition. Forty years was considered a 'grandfatherly' age at that time, but he had been 'free' to do so only after he had settled off all his sisters, and once he did, many of his students had insisted that he should think of starting a family of his own.

Once a week, guru and shishya went off to the movies together, sometimes taking a meal after the show. Datta-ji would then finally and reluctantly allow Pandit-ji to go home, for Pandit-ji would worry about what his father might say, as it would get late at night.

Datta-ji was only too aware of the circumstances in which Pandit-ji lived. He was particularly anguished about his level of nutrition. This was the period when Pandit-ji's throat had started bleeding after his riyaz—no less than seven to eight hours of non-stop practice. In any traditional gharaanaa, this rigorous routine called for a high protein and fat diet with non-vegetarian food, milk, lots of dry fruit, halva, or sweet semolina made in pure ghee and so on. One day, when Datta-ji could take it no longer, he placed an ultimatum before Pandit-ji. By that time, of course, Pandit-ji was earning a lot of money, for it was not just the regular AIR broadcasts that had provided him a respectable beginning to his musical career, but also the several tuitions that he would take regularly, at the homes of his students, where he was treated like royalty.

So Datta-ji insisted one day (threatened would be a better description), 'Look, son, leave a tin of ghee at the halwai's shop.' (Datta-ji lived on the first floor of a building, below which there was a halwai's shop.) 'As you come up to me every day, mix a spoonful of it in a glass of milk he gives you and have it. Or else I will no longer give you any lessons. For all the riyaz that you do, you will die on those boiled potatoes. And do not disclose this at home. You know I am saying this because you can afford it now.'

In contrast to his relationship with Datta-ji, sadly, over the years, the image that Pandit-ji had developed of Pita-ji was that of a spineless man. He often recounted a story of the continued disappointment that he felt about this. One day, after they had all settled well in Delhi, Pita-ji came to see him at the AIR office, without telling him in advance. Pandit-ji was immensely and pleasantly surprised, but just before he could warm up with emotion, Pita-ji started talking about how he was getting on in years. He wanted to sell his house in Janakpuri, where he had lived all these years after coming to India, property that had been given to him by the government in lieu of the properties they had lost in Pakistan. By now, Pandit-ji had learnt what to expect and understood immediately.

'I am ready to give you in writing that I have no claim, whatsoever, on your property, and you can divide the money between your other children as per your wishes. I know this is why you have come,' he said and proceeded to write and hand over the note there and then, even as his eyes smarted.

'No, no!' Pita-ji said, 'no, no, no. I will tear up this note.' But Pita-ji did not do that. He instead pocketed it quietly, evidently relieved, before leaving. Subsequently, the house was sold, and all of Pita-ji's children 'after Nath' were given their share of the proceeds, including his married sisters. Again and again, Pandit-ji was struck by the truth of what he had known all along, but the actuality of it always surprised him. The ostracism stalked him at every turn in life; only, he had refused to let it sink in, and had lived in an unreal world of faith in family and human relationships. Pandit-ji had borne so much, for so long, and kept on with his extremely innocent, positive nature. That is why, especially after Pandit-ji married, there were long wide gaps in his relationship with his paternal family. They did not meet often, but when they did, there would be tears and emotional reunions at first, but soon the underlying betrayal would surface, and fresh wounds would appear. Then they would fester for long, perhaps till the next reunion.

Another incident would haunt him for years and led to a famous bandish of his. Once when Pita-ji was admitted into the hospital for a gallstone operation, he had sent for Pandit-ji. Pandit-ji took the day off from Triveni (where he was teaching) and took his entire family to see Pita-ji. They sobbed, both father and son, and the others followed suit. Then, Mata-ji appeared and uttered, '*Hai hai, ladan raat aave te vichadan raat na aave.*' (Oh, oh, come the night spent quarrelling, but not the night of separation.) This really affected Pandit-ji; the words haunted him for a long time. Not long after, came his khayaal bandish in Jaijaivanti:

Bidhana aisee kabahoon na rachiye,
Jaame milan ki baat na rakhiye.
Ladan raat sau sau rachiye,
Par bichudan raat na ek rakhiye.

(Do not create a destiny,
In which there is no union,
Create a hundred nights of quarrel,
But not a single night of separation.)

The last nail in the coffin came one afternoon that marked another day of emotional turmoil. Pandit-ji noticed something strange about Pita-ji's behaviour. He was affectionate towards Pandit-ji's children and held them close to him, but only when Mata-ji was not around. The second she came back, he would release them like a child caught stealing from a jar of sweets. Pandit-ji was very affected by this, the fact that this differential treatment should extend beyond him, to his children as well, shocked him.

Even though Pandit-ji loved his kids immensely, being a family man, he was not that easily approachable even to his children at home. Even if it looked like you could talk to him, you couldn't. There were times when even his children used to ask for permission before speaking to him. It was, of course, all very respectable, this sense of distance but he was like this with everybody. You could not take him for granted. He guarded his privacy immensely. Somehow, he always managed to keep an invisible 'Do not disturb' sign on him all the time, which was his way of being with the world and also without it.

However, he was a different man with Datta-ji. Life with Datta-ji was idyllic. He would look forward to the evenings, so he could go to him, after long hours of the day spent doing his own riyaz. Pandit-ji scheduled his riyaz in such a way that it sounded like penance, when he recounted it. But as he always reassured us, he was so comfortable in his skin doing those hours. Adolescence then was riyaz all through, with little breaks like looking down the window and telling his sister how to win the game of 'stapu' she was playing with her friends, or taking his younger brother to a painter friend he knew, and suggest that he take lessons, if that interested him.

All his life, he never stopped practising after the morning 'riyaz'. The only difference is, it continued in his mind. He used to sit in the sun on the terrace for hours in winter, working on a new raga until it had bloomed completely in his mind, working on a new lyric until the words revealed deeper and deeper meanings, to his satisfaction. Some of his finest musical discoveries came to him while travelling, or just in the middle of the night, or while taking his evening walk.

There were five to six students who would come to learn from him in the evenings, so from 4:00 a.m., when he would get up to practise, till late in the evening, he would be singing. He was such a sadhak that till the last days of his life, the 4:00 a.m. routine had not changed one bit. Around this time, he formed the habit of taking a half-hour nap in the afternoons, sometimes even forty-five minutes, from which he regained his energies for the next half of the day.

That habit stayed with him for the rest of his life. His little afternoon nap became famous, especially amongst his students, and they would laugh that even if the prime minister was to visit Guru-ji, he would excuse himself from the meeting to go up to his bedroom for his afternoon nap, and return to start his next session of music after a cup of tea.

One would think that Pandit-ji would be bitter towards with his half-siblings but nothing could be further from the truth. Pandit-ji was a very giving brother; it came naturally to him and was perhaps connected to his eternal yearning to belong. He had already started performing at AIR, the youngest of the sixteen accredited musicians on the rolls, which included Ustad Bade Ghulam Ali Khan of the Patiala gharaanaa and Ustad Abdul Wahid Khan Saheb of the Kirana gharaanaa. Once he started earning, he promised to, and indeed financed, the education of his sister, and encouraged her to study. 'Study as much as you want, I will finance your education, all through high school and college as well. You go on studying.'

He kept his promise. He believed in his heart that his sister should not suffer the lack of a formal education, as he had. And so, it was natural that she became his devotee. She would sit up for him at nights after he came back from Datta-ji's and cook fresh rotis to go with what was cooked for dinner. She would make his breakfast after his first long stretch of morning riyaz. They were each other's strength to such an extent that Pandit-ji called her the Dorothy to his Wordsworth, supportive all the way.

* * *

Pandit-ji's wife, Maya, would often say, 'When I married him he resembled a patient of tuberculosis!' He was not, of course, but he looked like one, he was so lean. His face was so thin that his eyes looked larger than usual, accompanied by a look which carried a touch of the haunted in them. But Pandit-ji was very handsome, like the Hindi film heroes of his day. Some said he looked a lot like the actor Rajendra Kumar. He never thought about his looks however; he was so lost in the world of music that let alone external factors like how one looks, even a spell of fever did not stop him from his engagement with music. So much so that one day, in spite of being ill, when Pandit-ji heard that Ustad Amir

Khan, a musician he respected immensely, was coming down to Lahore for a concert in the city organized by the Punjab Music Society, he made sure he attended it. Pandit-ji was smitten by Khan Saheb's music, having heard him once over AIR, Lahore, and this was to be his first 'darshan' of the great master. There was of course a certain amount of trepidation, so he was also weak in the knees—the very thought of being able to set eyes on the person whose singing had been haunting him ever since he had first heard him.

Since he was feverish, he took a quilt along with him in case things went from bad to worse (which they did on that strange day). He sat on a seat in the last row of the auditorium, so as not to disturb, but also in case he needed to go away in the midst of things. But Ustad Amir Khan's music had a deep impact on Pandit-ji. So, he continued to sit there in rapt attention. Perhaps it was from the relief of having connected with what he had been looking for all the years of life he had lived till now. Or perhaps it was the fact that he was looking at the man who had been, as he said, his guru through many janmas or births, but for almost a fortnight after that night he could not touch his own taanpura— he was in a daze. Soon enough, he came down with a fever from which he was to emerge only after many weeks.

The story of Pandit Amarnath's days as Ustad Amir Khan Saheb's shishya is perhaps one of the most poignant in the annals of Hindustani music. 'When I first heard Khan Saheb, it was like taking a morphine injection—I was doped for days.' The guru–shishya chemistry was so profound that one day he said to Ustad Amir Khan: *'Main toh kayi janmon se aap ka shishya banta chala aa raha hoon.'* (I have been evolving as your disciple over many births.) As his younger guru bhai, Gajender Baxi, once said, 'Pandit Amarnath was Amir Khusro to Ustad Amir Khan's Nizamuddin Auliya.'

Ustad Amir Khan now became his 'dhyeya', as he once said, 'his point of concentration', and that spiritual journey—for which both 'ustad' and 'shagird' were born—began in Lahore before Partition, though he formally became his disciple in Delhi only in 1948, after the partition.

* * *

In Pandit-ji's life, Partition played a big role. Back in 1947, as they lived their lives in Lahore and as Pandit-ji apprenticed with Datta-ji, the tension in the air had become palpable. Their future in the little town became increasingly uncertain. A time came when they were no longer sure that all members of the family would collect together as usual in the evening after the traumatic events of each day. This was especially when riots would break out at the drop of a hat. So the family was forced to start thinking about their safety, and about the options before them, especially considering that they were Hindus. The last straw was the burning down of the Shalami darwaza, or Shalami Gate, a focal point of the town, close to where they lived, and it was time to take whatever few precious belongings one could and move to Hindustan before it was too late. Someone had to be found to facilitate this huge move. Rai Saheb, or Lala Chokananad Sindhwani, as he was known, was Pandit-ji's paternal uncle or Bua's son. He was in the railways, and it was he who helped them. Despite the deluge of people seeking entry into the trains, they were able to take the train to India. The family divided into two parts, with whatever possessions they could carry.

As far as Pandit-ji was concerned, he just picked up his one and only loved possession, his taanpura, put it into its cover, and was ready to travel, leaving behind not only an entire country, which he was never to visit again, but also the smells of the lanes and the neighbourhood he was brought up in. This included the Said Miththa at the Krishna Gali in Lahore, the Mitti puttan di gali, the Lohe vali gali, the Khajoor gali, and above all, that affectionate walk to Nisbat Road, where Datta-ji lived. This neighbourhood contained an entire childhood, along with its remembered, and forgotten, memories.

Pandit-ji was only twenty-three years old. For a few days, they were lodged as sharanarthis or refugees in a sea of camps in Delhi. Tents overflowing with people, each family struggling for water, food and the essentials of life while living with the trauma of having left everything behind, including property, wealth and their own extended families.

Without wasting any time, Pandit-ji went to the AIR station close to Parliament Street and was enrolled immediately as a classical artist on their rolls. Along with this, even as they were still in the camps, he resumed his riyaz, right there in the tents in which they now lived. The refugees in the camps admired him immensely, but some of the extended family was envious. So when Pandit-ji bought his first pair of clothes in India, two silk shirts and a pair of off-white trousers with the fees he received from AIR, there were many in the camps who accused him of 'doing much too well with the Partition', or as they said, '*Nath noon taa Partition raas aayaai.*'

Soon, Pita-ji found a job and was sanctioned a house at the Railway Quarters, in Kishanganj, near Delite Cinema, so the family was able to shift here from the camps and settle down all over again. Flat No. 27, on the first floor, had a small barsati where Pandit-ji went straight up and placed his taanpura, as if to say—'now this is our new home, yours and mine'. This is where he and his taanpura were to practise together for five more years, eight hours a day; far from the maddening crowd.

The one major change from the life in Lahore was that he no longer went to the homes of his students to teach. They came to him to learn, and life was more convenient for him now. A barsati had its own kind of life to offer, it sometimes burnt with the sunshine, it sometimes let all the rain in, but it was also independent and private, and he could internalize a lot, give himself over to a great deal of reflection, even as he remained a part of the run-of-the mill life of a family.

Apart from his musical practice this phase also taught him something entirely unrelated. Down below from his barsati, Pandit-ji could see the godowns of a retail shop where great big piles of pulses would dry in the sun, to be packaged and marketed. He observed minute details, like how the pulses were just about but not completely dried and were then marketed before they were ready. When he finally established his own home and family, he passed the order that each day, when the lentils were cooked, they should be boiled without the lid of the pressure cooker, and the froth that came up the surface should be removed first before they were prepared the usual way. He explained that it was because the pulses still retained some amount of moisture in them, which turned fungoid, and that this fungus came up to the surface when it started to boil.

While living a simple life with simple chores, Pandit-ji soon learnt of Ustad Amir Khan Saheb's place of residence—Ajmeri Gate. He gathered the courage to go there. Not once, but several times subsequently, Pandit-ji requested Khan Saheb to teach him, but Ustad-ji said that there was nothing to learn, and nothing to teach. He never seemed inclined. Eventually, one day, he told Ustad Amir Khan Saheb after yet another refusal that the day would come when he wouldn't ask, but Khan Saheb himself would request to teach Pandit-ji. Hurt, he then turned on his heels and left.

There were several tribulations in the relationship of the guru and the shishya. On one hand, Pandit-ji accepted Ustad Amir Khan Saheb as the father figure in his life, and as a result his children too began to accept him as their grandfather. He used to live with them for a few months in a year and continue on to other cities for concerts and other shows. Pandit-ji's family always believed that it was God who had come home to stay with them; such was the reverence. On the other, when Pandit-ji had asked Ustad Amir Khan for a particularly challenging pattern, the guru responded by giving him the complicated pattern for Bheem Palaasee: Maa Saa Gaa Paa, Gaa Maa Nee Maa Paa Saa, Paa Nee Saa Maa Gaa Re, Saa Nee Dhaa Paa Maa Gaa Re Saa. And the second: Gaa Maa Paa Nee, Saa Maa Gaa Gaa Re Saa, Nee Paa Nee Nee, Paa Maa Gaa Re Saa Nee Saa.

This consumed Pandit-ji. For the next two or three days, he practised incessantly but could not articulate the pattern just right, to the extent that his friend went to Khan Saheb and requested that he reveal the trick to Pandit-ji else the boy would die, not having eaten or moved from his efforts in three days. Khan Saheb told Pandit-ji to separate the Maadhyam or Maa in the beginning and join it later. It was done instantly.

While relating this story years later, Pandit-ji made it clear that it was not compassion that had made his guru reveal the trick to him, for there were several times when Ustad Amir Khan tested him to the hilt, beyond endurance. Like in the composition, '*Tu Jabbaar, tu Sattaar, hukam teraa*'. Pandit-ji used to say that in the matter of teaching, Khan Saheb was pitiless, like a butcher.

On yet another occasion, Pandit-ji took nearly fifteen or twenty days of unpaid leave to visit Khan Saheb in Bombay upon his request, believing that there would be something new to learn, something exciting. Khan Saheb would initially not even think of teaching him, and Pandit-ji would just listen to his guru sing.

One day, Khan Saheb began to teach Pandit-ji Darbaaree, '*He see beer see, jaa na mann chaahe*'. Of the three weeks, when there were only two days left, Pandit-ji requested that Khan Saheb also teach him the second half of the song but Khan Saheb simply said that it would be done on a subsequent visit.

Their love grew immensely to the point that sometimes Pandit-ji would also get annoyed with Khan Saheb. When Khan Saheb took to drinking quite a bit, neglecting his health and as a result spoiling his digestion, he was given medicine. He would have it only if it was personally fed to him. Every once in a while, when Khan Saheb would gauge that Pandit-ji was in a foul mood because of this, he would oblige slightly to appease him.

On the hundredth anniversary of Mirza Ghalib, the Government of India was to make a film in his honour. Pandit-ji was called in as music director, and it had been decided that Ustad Amir Khan Saheb would sing the title song. Pandit-ji was surprised that Khan Saheb was singing a ghazal, but he was told that Khan Saheb had consented.

On the day of the shoot, Khan Saheb had refused to sing. The whole team, including M.S. Sathyu the director, Abu Shivani the producer, was alarmed and Pandit-ji went to Ustad-ji's flat in Peddar Road with everyone, on condition that he and he alone would speak to his guru.

It turned out that Ustad Amir Khan Saheb had simply nodded at the idea during a drinking session, but had not actually agreed to it; after all, at his age, he wasn't going to sing a thumree or a ghazal. After a lot of cajoling, Pandit-ji explained that Khan Saheb had sung in Persian, Arabic and Hindi, so why should Urdu be punished? Besides, the ghazal had been composed in the original style of a century prior, and if Khan Saheb was still not happy with the composition, he could compose it himself, if it pleased him so. Knowing that in twenty-five years of apprenticeship,

Pandit-ji had never put a wrong foot forward, Khan Saheb finally consented.

Pandit Amarnath would often say that Ustad Amir Khan Saheb was not performance-conscious: 'He just sings. What you want—he will not pay any attention to that element. He will not produce "items". He will sing as though he is singing for himself, he is pleasing himself. And he was his own audience. He was his own listener. He would say, "If I sing to please myself, you are automatically going to be pleased."'

Thus, this is where the first important maxim of the now renowned style and approach of the gharaanaa of Indore developed, which Khan Saheb himself founded, the first abstract style in Hindustani khayaal music: *'Apne liye gaao'*—'sing for yourself'.

There were remarkable similarities between both guru and shishya. Both were sufis. Ustad Amir Khan traced his musical ancestry to the Qawwal Bachche gharaanaa of the time of Amir Khusro and Pandit Amarnath to the Sufis of Punjab, descendants of Baba Farid. In fact, Pandit-ji would proudly say that Jhang, his birthplace, was the hometown of many Sufi fakeers. It is interesting that while Khan Saheb sang taraanaas—spiritual poetry in Persian—Pandit-ji sang kafis—spiritual poetry in Punjabi— both giving utterance to the music of the soil to which their hearts belonged.

But their greatest contribution lies in the khayaal, whose scope and reach they changed forever in Hindustani music. As Pandit Amarnath explained ever so often, 'It was Khan Saheb who discovered the pause in music.' The pause represented anhada naada—the unheard music—which generated the heard music, the 'naada', and as his music wove uttered phrase with silent phrase, his singing, even as it enlivened the rich life of the here and the now, brought to the listener the music of the beyond.

Another musical folklore goes that one night after dinner, guru and shishya—Ustad Amir Khan Saheb and Pandit Amarnath—were taking a leisurely walk. Normally, Khan Saheb's silence would speak and communicate everything to the initiated and there would often be no need for a verbal dialogue. But this time his silence directed towards his shishya expressed that he wished to say something. Soon he stopped and said, 'My son, every night at bedtime you must hum the raga circling in your mind, before you sleep. If there is any doubt, keep thinking about it till you fall asleep. In the morning it shall have been resolved.' It was a guru-mantra that Pandit-ji would never forget.

* * *

The days spent at the barsati above Pandit-ji's father's house in Delhi were now coming to an end. This was because one day, just as life seemed was normal again, Pandit-ji discovered that it was not really so with Mata-ji, who kept a hawk's eye on his income and earnings. So, a debate over the amount he earned and the amount he gave to his father for expenses at home started. He started giving 100 rupees to Pita-ji, out of the 320 rupees that he received every month from AIR (he recorded four days a month, once each week, and received 80 rupees for each recording). But there was immense tension in the air, about him not contributing what he could well afford. One day he asked for an extra helping of something during dinner and she bitterly said, '*Sau rupaye ghar de ke teekda hai!*' (He gives 100 rupees home and kicks his heels!)

Pandit-ji was in no mood to go on with all this any more. He decided to move out. In Delhi, he had already become friends with Jaidev, who would later become a very well-known music director in the Bombay film industry. Jaidev too had run away from his ancestral home in Ludhiana and had come to Delhi.

Like Pandit-ji, Jaidev too was emotional and they both hit it off very well. Together, they found a small part of a house they could rent in Rohtak Road, Karol Bagh, a house that would become famous for the visits of Ustad Amir Khan Saheb and Ustad Ali Akbar Khan Saheb, their respective gurus.

They hired a servant, Sher Singh, who managed everything, cooking as well. Largely left to himself, Sher Singh benifited most from the goodies provided for in the kitchen, the milk and ghee, leaving very little nourishment for the two men who slaved all day to make ends meet. Jaidev-ji took tuitions; their more or less equal contribution to the monthly expenses was very hard earned. However, Sher Singh enabled them to have the independence and freedom to evolve as musicians and artists, for that was the whole idea in the first place.

Apparently, Pandit-ji joined the Gandharva Mahavidyalaya at some point as a guru, when it was lodged in what was known as Prem House in Connaught Place; and that could be true, for there were many links with Pandit Vinay Chandra Maudgalya. It was because of Pandit Maudgalya that Pandit-ji was lecturing and performing there, not only in the early years that he came to Delhi, but for long after that too. Soon enough, he was to join the staff of AIR, courtesy Pandit Ravi Shankar.

Pandit Ravi Shankar became another good friend. The friendship with Robu Da, which was what they used to call Pandit Ravi Shankar those days, had grown to the extent that Ravi-ji would be up at the barsati ever so often, and Pandit-ji would be over at Sardar Patel Marg, where Robu Da lived, at the house of the Bharat Rams. They first met there, in fact, for Pandit-ji was there twice a week for tuitions, but their interactions took place apart from the days of the tuitions as well.

Despite his forward-looking nature, Robu Da was deeply steeped in the values of the traditional musical culture of the gharaanaa, being the disciple of none other than Allauddin Khan Saheb, being his son-in-law as well. Although he had set his eyes far for the future, when it came to Hindustani music, Robu Da was very traditional and this was the reason that musically they both saw eye to eye a great deal. This was to the extent that Robu Da suggested that they do their riyaz together at home in the evenings. However, as far as practice was concerned, Pandit-ji too had been steeped, but in a different kind of culture, for decades together, and he just could not see imagine practising with the sitar.

But the upshot of the friendship was that Robu Da invited him to assist him at AIR as composer–supervisor, where Pandit-ji's job was to compose songs, write them, set them to music, as well as record them with the National Orchestra once every week. This was the 'Song of the Week', but he was also to record the 'Song of the Month', which was even more special an affair. Depending on its popularity, as well as listeners' requests, it would be repeated on AIR all the time, all day, all month, between other programmes.

Two of his songs became very big hits, remembered years after they first played over the airwaves. One was a song Pandit-ji had sung with Vinod Kumar, younger brother of Pandit Vinay Chandra Maudgalya, who was a well-loved exponent of the Patiala gayaki. The duet was '*Sajan bin roye, jogania hai Ram*'. It became so popular that even children on the streets would be found singing it. There was another duet, sung by Shanti Mathur and Shanta Saxena, two well-known voices in the Delhi of those times, '*Ja ja re badara ja, re*', composed in Jayant Malhar. This one became even more popular than the film songs of the time.

Pandit-ji and Jaidev shared a lot of music together. Above all, they heard each other practise for hours at end. They also shared their musical creations, for by that time Pandit-ji had begun composing his own bandishes or songs in different ragas. Jaidev, too, was grooming himself, composing songs for a future with Bombay filmdom.

Having no family, except for a sister, Ved, who too settled down in England after she got married, Jaidev used to fantasize how he would pass away into the other world. '*Oh Bhappe*,' he would exclaim, 'you know I will take a bath, put on my best kurta and pyjamas, dab on my best perfume, and welcome the next life like a gentleman. No depressing thoughts and also no one to bemoan my loss.' Strangely enough, many decades later, this is exactly how it happened.

Jaidev never married, lived alone through the good days and the bad, and when he breathed his last in a city hospital, they took him away directly to the crematorium, as there was no one to take the body home. He had kept his word, he had worked it out long ago in his mind, much before it had actually happened.

Jaidev's best known song, '*Allah tero naam, Ishwar tero naam*', sung by Lata-ji for the film *Hum Dono*, was actually composed in Rohtak Road, long before it was recorded in Bombay. Pandit-ji even went with Jaidev for the recording. As they both knew Lata-ji well, Pandit-ji suggested to her that in the final repeat of the refrain when she sang *Ishwar tero naam*, she could just extend a taan into the ati teep or extra-high register. This she did with such affection, and which sounded so brilliant, like a flash embellishment, that she told him she looked forward to singing for him too one day, which happened through the songs of *Garam Coat*.

Pandit-ji insisted that he was 'a poet before a musician', and wrote verse, songs really, from adolescence. His first song was in Behag, '*Jeevan ke suhane din*'. His friends loved it so much that one of them, Amar Kumar, promised him, 'If ever I make a film, you will be its music director.' *Garam Coat* was the first film he made in Bombay and Pandit-ji composed the music for this Balraj Sahni–Nirupa Roy starrer.

As a film, *Garam Coat* was in the traditional classic mould; it was based on a short story by the well-known writer Rajinder Singh Bedi, and can easily be categorized under the cinema that carried literature to celluloid. It is the story about how a middle-class family survives one month without the father's salary, which consists of a hundred-rupee note. The film unveils a hundred little moments of silent devotion and solidarity of the wife and children, all under stress, and weaves the magic of family life of the India of those days. Amar Kumar did make a beautiful film, the frames carried a unique sense of painting on celluloid. Although Balraj Sahni was to pair opposite Gita Bali initially, it was Nirupa Roy who eventually played the female lead. The scenes between the two were charged with deep emotion.

Lata-ji sang all the songs. The songs, five in number, stood out, especially '*Jogia se preet kiye dukh hoye*'. She liked the most famous of the songs, the Mirabai bhajan, so much that she featured it in the first album she brought out of her life's ten best songs—in an LP by HMV, and of course this made Pandit-ji very proud. In fact, Lata-ji tore up the cheque she received for singing those songs, saying, 'After many years of singing, these songs have moved me immensely. Yours is a cooperative venture, let this be my contribution towards the making of the film.' The words made front-page news in *Screen*, the well-known film tabloid of those days.

Right from Lahore, the friends with whom he used to move around were artists, future film-makers, leftists, poets and such. Among them were Balraj Sahni, who visited his home in Karol Bagh a lot, Amar Kumar, the well-known Marxist Tajwar Samri,

Amarnath Kalra and Prem Mohlajee, who started the India Classical Music Society in Chicago.

There is a story with Mohlajee during Pandit-ji's visit to Chicago many years later. Cutting through Chicago's vast suburban landscape, they were driving at ninety kilometres an hour, en route to the beautiful neighbourhood of Oakbrook. Fields of maize cobs swirled past on both sides of the road. Mohlajee was smiling away. At the back of the station wagon he was driving was a rare taanpura jodi or pair, brought all the way from India.

'Last week they had a tamboora festival in New York,' explained Mohlajee. 'People flew in from many cities to attend it. The tamboora recitals went on for hours, complete with agarbattis and the chanting of Om. Now let's see what they make of this pair!' he exclaimed.

True to his predictions, there was a flutter of excitement as the taanpuras emerged from their black cases for the evening's recital at the Mariott Hotel Music Room—a light brown pair, unpolished, with no inlaid ivory work, and coiled kharaj (bass) strings, especially borrowed from the veena to give an earthy resonance rarely heard in the instrument before. Piped a Canadian, 'Is this the only "orchestra" Pandit Amarnath will be using during the recital?'

By the end of the evening, there were several enquiries. The unusual sobriety of the pair had only fascinated the Americans further. And Mohlajee, proud about his temporary custodianship of the instruments, ended his vote of thanks that evening saying, 'Last, but not the least, this—er—"orchestra"—is not for sale.'

One of Pandit-ji's other friends, Marxist poet Tajwar Samri was ridden with poverty for most of the life he led in Delhi. For years, he would drop by in his bicycle in the afternoons, mostly after lunch. Pandit-ji's wife would rustle up something for him, as he was always famished and looked tired and exhausted, be it summer or winter. Paranthas, pickles and loads of gorgeous creamy curd were served to him. Tajwar Samri led a mysterious life. And though he edited a well-known magazine in Urdu which was full of robust political writings and poetry, he was an unusually unhappy man. His wife had left him for another man at some point, and he had raised his two children, a son and a daughter, all by himself, later even finding a new lady in his life. Suddenly this made him dye his hair for a while, which did not go down well with Pandit-ji, who once even muttered that this was not a very graceful thing to have done.

But the constant years of poverty took such a toll that a sense of gloom would hit Pandit-ji whenever his friend arrived. Despite everything—all the camaraderie and the solidarity between them—it was not enough to stall the sense of the tragic with every visit. Once when too many days had passed and he had not visited, Pandit-ji began to wonder. The possibility of Tajwar having passed away in some corner of the lanes of the city was not ruled out either. That was exactly what had happened.

Pandit-ji was told about it a few days later. A messenger came and narrated one of the gloomiest stories you could have heard about anyone. And yet, what redeemed the sad life of Tajwar Samri somewhat was another visit by the same friendly messenger, a while later, reporting that his daughter had now been married into a family where she was so ecstatically happy, it was hard to believe.

Pandit-ji was reminded of Tajwar's poem, which he had composed into a thumree, which has become a part of the repertoire of the Indore gharaanaa:

Kahe ree main ban-than aayyee,
Piya mann tanik na bhaayi,
Jab se khadi dekhat nahin balam,

nain agan bhadkaayee.
Kahe ree main ban than aayyee.

(Oh why did I come all dressed,
For pleased I not my Lord.
Before him, ever since I stood,
Not a glance gave me my beloved,
His eyes singed red with fire)

Another friend, Niaz Haider or Niaz Baba, was a confirmed bachelor. Typical Urdu adeeb (poet), he wore the kind of long coats that you associated with Mirza Ghalib, had a greying beard that reminded you of Rabindranath Tagore, and was extremely engaging in his demeanour. He was very vocal in his admiration and love for Pandit-ji. This was not new; people saw the savant in him from a very early period in his life, and there had been many before Niaz Baba, and there were to be many after him as well. The many women who loved him to the point of desperation were also all the same. Sometimes you could mistake it for the 'ishq' sort of love, though, in fact, it was the other, more reverential Sufi kind.

Niaz Baba would drop by in the evenings, and it was very natural that there would be drinking sessions and he would invariably end up sleeping the night over. He was a celebrated poet, one among the Progressive Writer's Association, which included Ali Sardar Jafri, Rajinder Singh Bedi, Kaifi Saheb, Majrooh Sultanpuri, Sahir Ludhianvi and actor Balraj Sahni.

Pandit-ji used to light-heartedly call his Marxist friends 'udhade huye log', 'people who had come apart', *udhada* being the word for a piece of cloth that 'comes apart' at the seams. But it is not torn clean; it is torn due to age. It was all about the difficult financial times they all faced.

Another story worth remembering is that of *Amrapali*. This was the well-known musical by Begum Qudsia Zaidi, who established Hindustani Theatres sometime during the year 1954. Her passion for theatre even won her a close admirer in Pandit Jawaharlal Nehru at an early age and with whom she remained friends for the rest of her life. She was an aristocratic lady of the arts and this was one of her early special productions—a big hit of the capital those days, running to a packed auditorium, Sapru House, for months.

The musical was a much-loved form of that period and Pandit-ji composed many songs for the play and also the background score. He loved the story of Amrapali and Ajatashatru, especially the scene in which two of the actors chanted, *Pak meri haandi pak pak pak, doodh ka pyala peene tak, pak, pak, pak*, while stirring a very large handiya or wok. The musical got him so many accolades, and lifelong admirers. One of these was Niaz Haider, a sort of a celebrity at the Indian People's Theatre Association (IPTA), who had scripted the musical. Niaz Haider would drop in unannounced at home for years to see Pandit-ji, another fixture like Tajwar Samri. Those were the days when Pandit-ji hardly ever socialized—so they all had to come home to see him.

Perhaps he found socializing a strain, or perhaps he did not have that kind of time on his hands, because even if he seemed to have spaces, he was mentally very preoccupied. His mind was always in the throes of composing some new bandish or the other, or working out the chemistries of a new raga he was handling at that time.

Coming back to *Amrapali*, Pandit-ji saw in the story the anguish of monkhood within the confines and involvements of family life, something that always rang a bell in him. He saw in the character of Amrapali a texture of mendicancy that he himself represented. *Yeh bhog bhi ek tapasya hai, tum tyaag ke maaro kya jaano*—those lines from a song in the 1966 version of the film touched him immensely every time he heard them, and he once mentioned that he had seen the film seventeen times when he was younger. This was, of course, the 1945 version of the same name, but he loved the later 1966 version as well, which starred Vyjayanthimala and Sunil Dutt, and reflected on it long after the screening of the film was over. In the silence of that reflection came to him an easy-flowing bandish in Shudh Kalyan, which if you once start singing, you will have to make yourself stop at some point, it will not stop of its own:

> *Sakal saaj, sakal aaj,*
> *Chhand rahe tumhare kaaj*
> *Saadhu ke mat anek, Jo saadhu moh kare,*
> *Ham to un mein se ek,*
> *saanchi kahat kaun laaja . . .*

Shishya Turns Guru

Back in the initial days, at the end of five years of learning, his first guru, Prof. B.N. Datta, whispered into Pandit-ji's ear: 'My only seva, or service, is that you teach music to everyone as I have taught you, without holding anything back, giving in abundance, for this is how this vidya or knowledge is meant to be passed on.' And on the first day of his 'ganda-baandh rasam' or sacred 'tying-the-thread' ritual of discipleship, his second guru, Ustad Amir Khan Saheb, whispered, as is the practice, into his ear: 'Do not give away this vidya or knowledge to anyone or everyone who asks for it. Give only to the rare and deserving—and that too only after the sacred ganda ceremony.'

It was at the age of sixty, one morning, as he lay recovering from an illness on a hospital bed that Pandit Amarnath, his eyes brimming over, discovered that both his gurus had said the same thing to him. The differences and contradictions had melted away—his gurus were now a single entity.

An important tradition in the gharaanas of Hindustani music is the practice of taking permission from your first guru if you want to move on to another guru during the period of learning. In the case of Pandit Amarnath, his first guru had actually said to him, 'Go to Ustad Amir Khan Saheb, I know your soul is craving for it, and for this, if need be, I will help and support you financially also.' For the great man knew the principles of continuity and connectivity in the guru tradition—that what changed were the face and the form and the name. What remained a constant was the guru.

In our own gharaanaa of Indore, the master guru, Ustad Amir Khan Saheb, was known to take forward his raga repertoire from fifteen or twenty, sung by his predecessor generation, to sixty to seventy, in his own lifetime. After him, his disciple Pandit Amarnath added another 200 ragas or so to this number, enriching the repertoire of the school even further, with new bandishes in those ragas. Both masters were also very bold in terms of introducing these lesser-heard melodies to an audience not yet initiated into the rigours of these bandishes. With each raga they were, after all, only evoking its blessings, for everybody and for themselves.

Pandit Amarnath often used to tell this story to his disciples. One morning, when the Kirana gharaanaa master Ustad Abdul Wahid Khan Saheb was singing Lalit at the dargah of Ajmer Sharif, the presiding pir saheb was moved to tears. As the pir saheb tried to gather more people around the master to hear him sing, he said something that can be said for all ragas when they are sung or played with devotion—'*Lalit ki khairat bat rahi hai, ise lete jao*', 'Lalit is being distributed as sacrament—prasad—please take it along with you!'

The road to creativity was a monotonous one indeed. Long hours of repetition, after which the ustad asked the disciple to repeat some more, because the swaras or notes had not yet been honed to a celestial shine. Repetition was the stuff life was made of. But behind the repetitions was the idea that the creative process was unleashed by the method of suffocation through sheer monotony.

In one of his lectures, Pandit-ji explained this technique as an expression of one of the highest principles of creativity. He illustrated his talk by asking one of his students to sing a 'palta' or exercise in a raga fifty times over. By the time she had managed to sing it seven to eight times, she changed the exercise a bit, on her own, just out of the desire to escape from the monotony. He asked her to stop then and there—'Enough, this is all I wanted!' No wonder that Pandit-ji was totally against the 'rationalization' of the process of learning Hindustani music in the universities of the country.

Pandit-ji's students found each day a challenge to be with the master; he would undo your mental conditioning until you discovered your own spiritual core. What Pandit-ji took you to, over and over again, was shunya or nothingness, the shunya of the Sufi drained of all notionhood—not empty but full, where nothing remained but the spirit. 'Shunya ho kar gaao,' he would say to them.

'Shunya', the natural state for meditation, for inner laya, took Pandit-ji himself to an inebriated state when he sang. One of his students once said, 'Guruji gaate nahin hain, gote lagate hain'. Guruji does not sing, he takes holy dips in the river within.

Like in meditation, the Indore style flowers at the base of the voice, also in keeping with the traditional principles of raga exposition. During a morning concert in New York in 1986, where Pandit-ji was singing Todi, he opened his eyes in the course of the recital and said, '*Hindustani raga aadha seekhne ki zarorat hoti hai.*' You need to learn only half the Hindustani raga. It was a profound statement, for while the maximum number of ragas bloom in the poorvang or first half of the raga, the uttarang or second half—as its name suggests—is an answering part and improvisation here is repetitive in nature.

Next in importance in understanding his style is merukhand, the warp and woof of the style—'meru' means spine, 'khand' means parts. Merukhand, also mentioned in the twelfth century *Sangeet Ratnakara* by Pandit Sharangadeva, is used by the Indore masters to carry their aalaap and taan forward. Ustad Amir Khan used the merukhand formulae of permutations and combinations of swaras in a revolutionary manner. Though the merukhand approach has been qualified as scholarly, it has created striking note combinations in Khan Saheb's music and unravelled the rare permutations in the music of Pandit Amarnath.

Once, at a concert and lecture demonstration at India International Centre someone asked him to explain merukhand briefly. Pandit-ji roared, 'You want me to reveal to you my forty years of tapasya in merukhand in just four minutes? How can I?' What he meant was that you had to climb the mountain yourself to know its parts. The journey was 'sadhana', 'siddhi' and 'samadhi', in that order.

Khan Saheb taught the merukhand to his students, its applicability in each raga was for the student to figure out on his own. This was how Pandit Amarnath-ji received his taleem, all of which he then himself intelligently processed to make the hundreds of secrets and principles of the gaayakee available in a systematized form for the next generation.

However, doing exercises in merukhand is one thing, their application in the rendering of the raga is quite another. In the traditional taleem of the Indore gharaanaa, both that which Khan

Saheb's father Ustad Shahmir Khan gave to Ustad Amir Khan as well what Ustad Amir Khan gave to his students or disciples, the emphasis was on developing an immense agility with the swaras that made almost any and every creative turn possible in music.

When Khan Saheb taught merukhand exercises, his way was to question his students about their applicability or applications in specific ragas. Only a very sophisticated student could work out those applications and be able to evoke a semblance of Khan Saheb's gaayakee into his own singing style. However, when Pandit Amarnath evolved his method, based on a set of ten seed exercises or bija paltas as we call them, which were to be sung in every raga, they were framed in a way so as to become directly applicable to the final rendering of the raga, both vilambit, madhya and drut.

What is unique about the exercises is that they are formulated so as to develop the raga and not its scale, which is what the merukhand exercises do initially. Another interesting difference is that the merukhand exercises are not based on the Indore gaayakee, Pandit Amarnathji's exercises are. That was also done to deliberately cut down on the time to be spent in apprenticeship, by almost half, because there was no unnecessary time spent doing scales that were not applicable to the raga.

In fact, the biggest secret which Pandit-ji told us was that the enlightened eye of Ustad Amir Khan, for the first time, opened merukhand in the aavrohi—descending order of the scale—though Sharangadeva explains merukhand in the aarohi—ascending order. Pandit-ji gave us the clue, 'The aarohi does not contain the aavrohi but the aavrohi contains the aarohi. Going does not contain return but return contains going and that is how Khan Saheb transformed merukhand from a science into a philosophy.' His vision had come whole; he had seen the merukhand mandala.

Interestingly, the more the Indore masters perfected the art of the slow khayaal, the more they perfected the art of the drut or fast, and the principle here was that fast was a heightened form of slow that would look after speed naturally. Speed for its own sake—which some instrumentalists are wont to do to 'prove' themselves—was self-destructive. It destroyed the effect of any assiduously built-up aalaap.

However, Pandit-ji's approach in vilambit and drut was consonant, and he is perhaps the only musician who actually even composed jodas or pairs of compositions for the vilambit and drut parts of the same raga. Vilambit bol—or lyrics—matching drut bandish, the drut bol matching the bandish in vilambit.

In his last days, one of the most stunning observations he made about the khayaal as a form was, 'Slow to fast? It is only a mental image. There is fast to slow also, in form; you move from destruction to creation again . . .' That is also why he, like Khan Saheb, could easily slip into a deep vilambit, again a rare feat in the performing of ragas. Ultimately, theirs is an immortal music in that it gives a cyclic, and not a linear exposition, of the khayaal.

Pandit-ji became the rarest of rare musicians with his extraordinary sense of moorchhana, or the awareness of many musical scales when rendering a particular scale, which was his darshan of the virat in his singing. As a result, he sang a moorchhana-ang khayaal, which also led to his discoveries of many new ragas. Starting with Amarkali, he discovered for the paramparaa the ragas Odav Asavari, Shyam Bhoop, Gunaranjani, Kafi Malhar, Maru Basant and renamed Pancham Kalyan, from its moorchhana of the note Pa, in Puriya Kalyan.

Teaching is composed of both method and technique. Techniques evolve out of experience, and become the mark of a teacher's maturity over time. But a teaching method is, again, developed by a genius performer, which is then emulated by generations of teachers over time. For example, in theatre there is the Stanislavsky method of acting and the Grotowski school of acting. In the same way, we now have the Pandit Amarnath method of teaching/singing, which has come a long way from the traditional classical teaching method in a number of ways.

When Pandit Amarnath-ji evolved a unique teaching methodology for the gaayakee of the Indore gharaanaa, he taught hundreds of students in his own lifetime, but as a student himself, it was not an easy road when he learnt from his guru, Ustad Amir Khan Saheb. This was because Ustad Amir Khan Saheb did not come down to the level of the student to teach. You had to be both humble and develop a questioning power equal to the musicianship of the master. You had to reach his level to learn.

Pandit Amarnath also felt that in all the music syllabi in the universities and elsewhere, not a single examination paper was devoted to the khayaal bandish as a poetic-musical genre. This was despite the consensus amongst musicians that the old bandishes were 'eyes' to the ragas, in that they were very valuable for having preserved the older and sometimes very profound interpretations of the ragas.

Apart from this, very little attention was paid towards its poetic content. It may be added that during the period 1985–88, Pandit Amarnath-ji took up a project on the subject of gharaanaa taleem or training as well as the system of syllabus-based training of Hindustani music under the university system in the country for the Indian Council of Social Science Research. It is one of the most outstanding analysis of the teaching of Hindustani music in the gharaanaa and university systems ever undertaken, but went unpublished due to its controversial nature.

The Poet and the Thinker

Pandit-ji blazed a new trail in the lyric of the khayaal in the twentieth century. He matched the antarmukhi gaana or inward-faced singing of his gharaanaa with antarmukhi bol, or inward-looking lyrics, extending his gharaanaa repertoire from sixty to over 200, in the process creating a new chapter in the Sufi history of the khayaal.

He pioneered many a lost cause in the history of the parampara, post the feudal period, both for Hindustani music and for the Indore gharaanaa in the twentieth century. As a musicologist, he reinterpreted the hidden meanings of esoteric ancient texts to make them accessible for the layman. In this aspect, he truly lived the life of a nada yogi, and showed by personal example.

The bandishes came to him at high moments of revelation, *jab haal chadhta hai*. There was always some external inspiration, of course, that escalated him to this peak of samadhi, when the subconscious mind spoke. Traditionally, these divine moments have been called vaak, or the coming of the vakya, or saying of the saint, also called khayaal in classical music parlance. Pandit-ji used to say that it was a state of masti, when his face went flush with the meditation, and the connectivity with the divine energy. He used to look like he had taken an internal bath in some golden holy water—he looked so beatific, almost intoxicated, in ecstatic bliss.

That state would go on for some time, and the lyric would also keep coming to completion. Pandit-ji has also spoken of instances when the asthai and antara came to him at separate times. Once he had got the new mukhada or bandish, for the next two to three days he would be totally preoccupied with it. He would be finalizing the raga movements and perfecting each little detail, in an obsessive way and this would go on, say another two or three days more. Then the composition was ready to be noted in the diary and he would be at peace.

This was a kind of bittersweet pain to bear and Pandit-ji's views on pain were equally radical. Pandit-ji would always tell his disciples that it was necessary to learn how to endure pain; he would use the word *sehna* in this context. He, who received it, must bear it. And so he came to compose in Vibhas raga:

Kar saadhana, bhar yaatana,
Tript hoye sab sur kaamana.
Bhaavana taapas gulaab si,
Ur kantak bhar, jagat lubhaavana,
Kar saadhana.

(Be in sadhana,
Offer your appeal to the Lord.
Be like the mendicant rose,
Who, with a throat full of thorns, enchants the world
Be in sadhana)

In this bandish or composition he would often point out—has the world ever seen the rose as a tapasvi or mendicant, whose throat, filled with thorns (here the musician himself), spreads its aroma in the world. So intense was Pandit-ji's saadhana that he would say that the desire in today's musicians for name and fame was a sign of escapism; an inability to bear the pain that came with the sadhaana. No wonder, peace would ever elude them.

His body of work consists of over 250 khayaal compositions in various ragas in the genre that is well-known as the khayaal bandish, or lyric for the khayaal. Pandit-ji's bandishes came to be 'revealed' to him in the highly charged moments of his life, over an entire lifetime. Sometimes he would wait for years for a song to be completed, when an asthai or first part of the lyric would 'come to him', as it did in Eman with decades of space in between.

About this, he would tell another of his favourite stories. 'Oh, the "mukhada" (first line of the lyrics) of that one came to me in Pakistan, Lahore, in the 1930s . . . um, let me see.'

He ri sajani saanjh saloni aayi,
Kar kar shringaar, chalo piya ke dwar,
Chalo man ki aas ab leho pujayee . . .

(O my friend, comes the beautiful dusk,
Let us bedeck ourselves and go to the home of our beloved,
And slake the thirst of our hearts)

'At that time it was just a momentary emotional outburst, but I dumped it somewhere in my mind, to call back when I would come across that same "saanjh saloni", or beautiful dusk again. Then, on my way back from Indore to Delhi once, the train stopped at a small station in Ratlam. I, alone in the compartment, looked out of the window at a huge oak tree, and the song proceeded from where it had left off twenty years before, as I broke journey to complete it under the canopy of that tree.'

Meet milan ke akulane,
Jug beetan laage,
Jaage bhaag suhaag, pujao,
Gao, nit rang raaga,
Tore man ki baat ban aayee.
He ri sajani saanjh saloni aayi.

(Ages began to pass by,
As we longed for Union,
Then destiny awoke,
To celebrate our marriage.

So let us sing the colours of the ragas,
For our hearts' desires have come true)

In Raga Saparda Bilawal, he composed and sang this bandish, in
the jogi spirit yet again:

Soone jogia,
Rab son badi preet maan le.
Jap le sakal dinaan,
Jeevan jogia . . .

(O you lonely monk,
Take love to be greater than God.
Each day,
Chant the name of Life itself)

He echoes similar thoughts in Raga Kafi Kanhada:

Arre o re jogi,
Preet naa bhogi?
Tarsat sakal dinan,
Nahin daata ke man karuna upji,
Arre o re jogi . . .

The words or bol are a little satire on the yogi who does not believe
in journeying the spiritual path with a beloved, by a Sufi who
believes that the yaar or beloved is the true karuna or compassion
of God himself. To translate:

O yogi,
You did not experience love?
All your days were filled with longing,

And no mercy had He upon you?
O yogi . . .

It was Pandit-ji's belief that a song is the heart and the soul—the emotion and spirit—and the actual heritage of a civilization, about the spirit of the people, of how people think and love. No wonder, woven into its textures is always the theme of the beloved, without whom no song can be composed.

In a beautiful poem, Pandit-ji writes of how the geet and the meet, the song and the beloved, are born—in a presence of the absence of the beloved:

> When nobody listens, there comes a song
> When somebody listens, a beloved is born.
> In a hundred ways a song is born
> In only one way a beloved is born.
> When it is difficult to reach the other side
> A song is born
> When somebody comes from the other side
> A beloved is born.
> When somebody does not see through my eyes
> A song is born
> When somebody sees through my eyes, a beloved is born.

A song is so spiritually charged that the beloved transcends to The Beloved. In Sufism, the relationship between God and the beloved is fascinating for this reason. The beloved is the symbolic earthly route to the Beloved, the emphasis being not so much on the route as much as on the destination, where lies the noor or the eternal light divine.

Pandit-ji described spirituality as 'the unconditional decisions of the mind', when antar-dhyana or the concentration within helped the mind to reach absolute truths which were not anchored or conditioned by the external conditions of life. In music he translated this antar-dhyana into antarmukhi gaanaa or a singing whose face was turned inwards, giving way to antar-darshan or a continuous unfolding of an inner vision when the khayaal was sung.

At this stage, the musician became a witness to his own singing, where, as Pandit-ji often said, '*koi meri aankh se dekh raha hai*'—'somebody is seeing through my eyes', and '*koi mere suron se gaa raha hai*'—'somebody is singing through my swaras, my notes'. This happened when your own personality did not intrude upon the laya or uninterrupted communication being experienced with the soul. When ragas were sung in this state of masti or self-intoxication, they became prasad or sacrament, showered by the inner-entity deity in laya.

Pandit-ji's countless bandishes or lyrics for the khayaal too have come from these 'self-charged' states of prayer, as he was wont to call them, the haal of the Sufis. In Raga Durga, Pandit Amarnath-ji sings of this by first asking a question, and then answering it himself:

How do I believe the Formless exists?
He has no land, nor a face,
Neither a form, nor a body.
How do I recognize the indications?
Oh yes, the formless himself becomes the form,
Takes on a body, and starts to love,
And, says the poet Miturang, upon this, all understand.

Miturang was Pandit-ji's pen-name, and he fondly called his grandson Mitu at home, though for the world he had been named Kabir—another of Pandit-ji's loves. He abundantly celebrated the concept of the mitwa through a hundred different nuances of approach. He recharged Sufi poetry for the khayaal and lifted it from its bairan saas-nanadiya or 'wicked mother-in-law and sister-in-law' modes to the level of Sufi soul.

In this context, a refreshing chapter is opened in the Sufi thought process of the subcontinent, in the form of khayaal lyrics penned by Pandit Amarnath, lyrics which improvise, in a riot of colours and hues, the theme or motif of the mitwa or soulmate—in the framework of another riot of ragas and raginis. The coming of the mitwa is symbolic of the end of existentialism, of existential angst. The cosmic has stirred . . . as a release after lifetimes spent in the dark karmic cycles of attachment and confinement.

In the khayaal bandishes of Pandit Amarnath, the mitwa is the Cosmic itself, an active proof of its infinite kindness and interest in you. In Kaunsi Kanhada, he says:

> You took on a form,
> You took on a name,
> The mitwa took on an avatar—a 'divine birth',
> To make the temple of my heart his home.

In Raga Saraswati, the mitwa speaks to you as your own reflection. The nayika or heroine says:

> O mitwa, listen to my heart.
> Since I became yours,
> I became my own as well.

As the beloved, she has found her real—her spiritual—identity. In Raga Shree, the poet says:

> One form of the Cosmic pervades my heart,
> Which is endless and of the Beyond.

As the formless, it be God, paramatma,
And as the form, be it the mitwa.

The mitwa will never fail you. In Raga Janasammohini, Pandit-ji
says:

Remember always him,
Whose remembrance brings ultimate joy.
For he whose feelings I bear in my heart,
Will come of his own, to enquire of me.

In two bandishes in Raga Gauri, the poet mulls over the strangeness
of fate and predestined human pain. In one:

Evening, and the branches twitter,
No branch stands alone.
Carries no nest the pain (of separation).
I wonder about this, again and again.

In the other:

Fly away, O bird,
So little is left of the day.
All the birds have their nests and homes,
In my destiny alone lies pangs of separation.

The chirping birds only echo the dark dungeons of separation, in
which the poet lives out his destiny in the Cosmic Weave. The
poet, however, knows how to solve the anguish:

Appears the mitwa in darshan (as vision)
As I meditate.

In Marwah, the beloved raga of his Indore gharaanaa, Pandit-ji consoles himself:

The dusk descends
In all four directions.
Where are you, O mitwa?
I stand at the door of meditation, for you,
Carrying the raga of my heart.

This teaching had a special appeal not only for students of music but also of theatre, that is, students of the voice, especially abstract theatre. Over the years, Pandit-ji also taught the disciples of Grotowski or Godowsky, pioneer of the abstract theatre movement in Europe, who in turn had discovered in the special voice culture of the Indore style a methodology that not only helped unveil the 'inner' voice but also one that offered another definition of immortality.

So, it can be surmised that the Sufis, whose poetry and music much influenced that of Pandit-ji's, were his masters. Like the true Sufi, he saw no great divide between the world and God, and preferred to see the world as God, inside which churned the ever-enduring cycles of ecstacy and pain.

Throughout his life, Pandit-ji campaigned for the cause of the lyric or 'khayaal' poetry as a genre that should be recognized both by the musicians as well as the poet fraternities of our land. The tragedy he said lay in poets not taking it seriously as an art form. 'The word loses consciousness of the word in the lyric,' he would say, and drops its weight, making it even more profound.

Once on the stage, Pandit Amarnath would ask for the overhead lights to be dimmed so their garishness would not disturb his 'samadhi'. He would, on the other hand, ask for dim lights to be switched in the hall where his audience sat, so that there would be no alienation between him and them and he could feel their warmth. He would ask for the echoes or reverb to be switched off in the speakers because according to him, 'It disturbs my thinking in the raga if I have to listen to my own pervious phrases.' It was actual meditation each time, each concert an 'avahan' or 'evoking' of the deity of the raga, a 'pooja'.

Even the most uninitiated in music felt deeply stirred by his presence and music. Along with his music, Pandit Amarnath will be remembered as a messiah of love in the great Sufi poetry that he wrote and set to music for the khayaal. He gave a fresh lease of life to both the khayaal lyric and the tradition of Sufi poetry.

'Yeh fikraa apne ko sunaao, phir dekho kaisaa lagtaa hai'— sing this phrase for yourself, and then see how it sounds, the Indore masters tell their disciples when they teach. So you can judge your music through your own inner mirror—the guru within—while striving for greater and greater truth in your singing.

Writing about Pandit Amarnath in the *Times of India* in 1996, the well-known critic Dr Raghava Menon said that the last of the four 'greats' of Hindustani music in the twentieth century had passed away. Ustad Amir Khan, Bade Ghulam Ali Khan and Pandit Kumar Gandharva had gone already, and now Pandit Amarnath. What is truly phenomenal is that two of the names he mentioned belonged to the same gharaanaa—the Indore gharaanaa—and were, in fact, guru and shishya.

* * *

Pandit-ji did not consider his voice just an instrument; he considered it his ears, his musical mind, the mirror of his inner life. 'My voice is the measure of my health—if that is okay, my body is okay,' he said. Pandit Amarnath composed the following poem in Poorvi, as a mirror to his spiritual dialectic with the world—when the world got too much for him, he would retract to his taanpura, forget everything and return to his ragas, and to the final source of solace he had—his inner self.

Ham so raho naa jaaye,
Baat naa boojhe koi,
Ye to jagat niraalaa.
Gehri saanjh ghir aayi,
Chale re meet ghar aapno,
Jit har pal aalaa.

(It is a strange world.
Difficult to understand,
Or endure.
A deep dusk encircles . . .
Come, my friend,
Let us return home (to the self),
Where each moment will be haloed)

He was a complete musician—fondly described as a 'musician's musician'. He was a vageyakar and composer, a great performing artist, a great teacher and margadarshak, not only for his students but also for all who came into contact with him. Not just that, he was a composer of music for films, a poet, a thinker and researcher whose lecture demonstrations are remembered all over the world. Above all, Pandit-ji was a savant, who opened a new chapter in the world of Sufi thought in the subcontinent, with unique bandishes he discovered for the Hindustani khayaal.

The work of a genius is always immensely complex and takes an entire lifetime to understand, whether by a disciple or a follower. Pandit-ji tried to make it easier for generations ahead to try and understand the world of classical music and thus created this unique compendium of musical terms—a torchlight for lovers of music. As a daughter who loved him and his music, I have the faith it will prove to be just that.

A

Aabhog: From bhuj, meaning to fulfil. Aabhog refers to that which has been absorbed completely. Here, it refers to the concluding part of a composition in dhrupad and dhammaar (see *Dhrupad*).

Aadee raga: Aadee means 'primordial'. Aadee ragas were the earliest ragas of the classical system. In general usage aadee raga refers to the basic or parental raga (see also *Janak raga* and *Upraga*).

Aadee taal: See *Taal*.

Aardh: From rdh, meaning 'to move'. Aardh literally means 'to move with obstruction'. Refers to continuous use of off-the-beat or 'odd' laya (a Punjabi word, ardhnaa, conveys the same meaning).

Aadhaa chautaal: See *Taal*.

Aahad: From aahat, which means 'that which is hurt'. Aahad is any physical effort that produces sound. Conceptually, this differs from anhad (see *Anhad naada*).

Aakaar: Singing with open mouth, pronouncing 'aa' (as in 'far', in other words, singing 'aa'-wise).

Aalaap: From aalaapnaa, meaning to spread. The contemplative unfolding and development of the raga which includes badhat, bol aalaap, behlaavaa (and in dhrupad-dhammaar, the tom-nom aalaap also).

Aamad: Any skilful entry, with an artistic phrase, into the orbit of the sam.

Aandolan: Literally, 'swing'. Refers to a swing between two adjoining notes. Certain notes in certain ragas are applied in this characteristic manner.

Aans: Haunting perfection of swara, and its finest lingering resonance.

Aarohee-avrohee: Aarohee comes from the word aaroh, meaning to ascend. The aarohee refers to the ascending order of notes in a raga. Avrohee comes from the word avroh, meaning to descend. The avrohee is the descending order of notes in a raga.

Aartee: A prayer song sung before a deity.

Aasaa-dee-Vaar: Aasaa is one of the deshee ragas from Punjab. Aasaa-dee-Vaar are certain verses from the Guru Granth Sahib (holy book of the Sikhs), sung in Aasaa in the mornings in gurudwaaraas (see also *Shabad, Deshee Sangeet*).

Aavart: From vritt, meaning 'to realize within', through (repetitive) practise'. Musically, any pattern of taan or tukraa of taal falling into the sam which has specific possibilities for repetition.

Aawaaz kaa jada pakarnaa: Aawaaz is 'voice', jada is 'root'. Refers to the voice being firmly established in its base. Generally, this phrase is used during kharaj (lower octave) saadhanaa, or practice.

Abdul Karim Khan: Great master of the Kirana school (1872–1937), popular because of his sweet and melodious voice. He sang mostly in ragee (half-tone). A master of the khayaal and thumree, he was especially fond of rendering sargam in the Carnatic style. His disciples were Sawai Gandharva, Roshanara Begum, Kapileshwari Bua, Dashrath Bua Maule and Ganesh Ramchandra Behre Bua (see also *Kirana gharaanaa*).

Abdul Wahid Khan: Great master of the Kirana school (died 1949), also known as Behre Wahid Khan, for his hearing was poor. A master of improvisation (badhat), he left behind many disciples: Hirabai Barodekar, Saraswati Rane, Suresh Babu, Firoz Nizami, Shakur Khan (who was a well-known saarangee player), Prannath and the Mattoo family. He died in Kirana (near Saharanpur, Uttar Pradesh) at the age of seventy-eight (see also *Kirana gharaanaa*).

Abhang: Devotional song-form, with lyrics in Marathi, composed mostly by saint poets like Namdev, Tukaram and Eknath.

Achal swara: Achal means 'immovable'. In the ashtak or octave, the two notes Saa and Paa are achal swaras. But in the saptak—or by the seven-note theory—only Saa is the achal swara.

Adarang: Pen name of Feroz Khan, khayaal composer in the court of Mohammad Shah 'Rangeele' (who reigned during 1719–

1748). All the compositions of Adarang available today reflect Sufi thinking (see also *Sadarang*).

Adaayagee: From adaa, which means 'personal style and cultivated manner'. Refers to the overall manner of presentation.

Agra gharaanaa: Well-known gharaanaa whose musicians are supposed to be descendants of Tansen from his daughter's side (her name was Saraswati). The characteristics of this gharaanaa are dhrupad-based khayaal, tom-nom aalaap before rendering of asthaayee and open-mouthed aakaar; a noteworthy achievement of this gharaanaa is that the musicians are known to sing even rare ragas with clarity and ease. The stalwarts of this gharaanaa have been Ustad Ghulam Abbas Khan, Nathan Khan, Bhaskar Bua, Faiyaz Khan and Vilayat Hussain Khan.

Ahmad Jan Thirakwa: Tablaa wizard of his time (1878–1976), also known as Thirakwa Khan (thiraknaa means 'to thrill'), he was a disciple of Munir Khan of Meerut. 'Thirakwa' was a title he earned in childhood, for the great dexterity of his fingers as they moved on the tablaa. Thirakwa Khan was court musician at Rampur, and associated with Maurice College, Lucknow, and Bal Gandharva's theatre troupe, the Gandharva Natak Mandali.

Ajrada: See *Poorab baaj*.

Akaal: Kaal is time, and akaal is, literally, 'out of time'. Musically, it refers to the showing of the sam deliberately out of beat (see also *Sam*).

Alankaar: Literally, 'ornament'. In general any phrase that beautifies the music; used mostly for paltaa or bal.

Ali Akbar Khan: Son and disciple of Allauddin Khan (founder of Maihar gharaanaa of music), Ustad Ali Akbar Khan (1922–2009) was a great musician and master of sarod. He spread Hindustani classical music at an international level. He composed several classical ragas and film scores. His prominent disciples are his sons Ashish Khan and Alam Khan, Ken Zuckerman, late Sharan Rani Backliwal, late Nikhil Banerjee and Tejendra Narayan Majumdar.

Alla Rakha: Ustad Alla Rakha (1919–2000) was a tablaa maestro who also specialized in Hindustani classical music. He was a disciple of Mian Kader Baksh of the Punjab gharaanaa of tablaa. He studied voice and Raag Vidya under Ashiq Ali Khan of the Patiala gharaanaa. He made a major contribution to the tablaa repertoire and basically set the paradigm dynamics of tablaa solo presentation. He had a long working partnership with Pandit Ravi Shankar. His sons Zakir Hussain, Taufiq Qureshi, Fazal Qureshi and his other disciples, Yogesh Samsi, Aditya Kalyanpur, Prafulla Atthlye, Navin Gandharva are prominent in the field today.

Alladiya Khan: Great master of the Kohlapur (Atrauli or Jaipur) gharaanaa (1855–1946). The special feature of his gaayakee was the prominent use of tempo throughout his rendering.

Though a Muslim, Alladiya Khan was a staunch Rajput, and wore the *janeoo* (sacred thread of the Hindus). His disciples were his two sons Munji Khan and Bhurji Khan, Kesarbai Kerkar, Bhaskar Bua Bakhle, Mogubai Kurdgekar, and Shankar Rao Sarnaik (known as Maharashtra Kokila); (see also *Jaipur gharaanaa*).

Allauddin Khan: Great sarod maestro of the twentieth century (1862–1972), also known as 'Baba'. Born in Tripura, he learnt from, among many others, Ustad Wazir Khan of Rampur. He settled in Maihar (Madhya Pradesh), where his reputation grew as a great teacher, his celebrated disciples being Ravi Shankar, Ali Akbar Khan, Annapurna, Pannalal Ghosh, Nikhil Bannerjee, Timir Baran, and many more.

Aman Ali Khan: Master of the Bhendi Bazar gharaanaa of Bombay (1884–1953). After Ustad Abdul Karim Khan, Ustad Aman Ali had a special knack for using khatkaas from the Carnatic style of rendering in his gaayakee. He was a gifted composer; the beautiful khayaal compositions in the raga Hamsadhvani—'*Laagee lagan satee patee sang*' and '*Jai maat, vilamba taja de*', are typical examples. Aman Ali Khan emphasized more on the Merukhand system in his khayaal gaayakee, a rare practice of that time (see also *Bhendi Bazar gharaanaa*).

Amir Khan: Great master of the Indore gharaanaa (1912–1974), Amir Khan was widely acclaimed for his unique, detailed raga vistaar (elaboration) and brilliantly conceived progression of taan patterns based on the Merukhand system. He also revived a version of the taraanaa (see also *Taraanaa* and *Indore gharaanaa*).

Amir Khusro: Famous poet–musician of the thirteenth century (1253–1325) and court poet to eleven emperors including Allauddin Khilji, Amir Khusro was the disciple of the Sufi saint Hazrat Nizamuddin Auliya. Khusro, who belonged to the Quwwaal Bachche tradition, is widely acclaimed for his contributions to both Indian classical music and poetry. He is associated with the evolution of the qawwaalee, khayaal, khamsaa and naat forms in singing; and among instruments the dholak and the sehtaar (which later developed into the sitar). The soolfaakh (asool-e-faakhtaa) taal is also attributed to him.

Amjad Ali Khan: Born on 9 October 1945 to sarod maestro Haafiz Ali Khan, Ustad Amjad Ali Khan is a renowned master of sarod. He received his training from his father. He is best known for his clear and fast ekhara tans. His disciples of note include Mukesh Sharma, Gurdev Singh, Vishwajit Roy Choudhary, Abhik Sarkar, Dev Jyoti Bose, Late Pramod Shankar, and sons, Amaan Ali Khan and Ayaan Ali Khan.

Ang: Literally, 'part'. In music, this refers to style; for example thumree ang, khayaal ang, tappaa ang, raga ang are used when a peculiarity of one style or raga is found in others. For example, it can be said that Gunkalee, Vibhaas and Raamkali are Bhairav ang ragas.

Anhad Naada: Naada is sound—here, musical sound that is not heard by the physical ear. Often used to refer to music felt within (compare with the English unheard).

Annapurna Devi: Annapurna Devi (1927–2018), daughter and disciple of Baba Allauddin Khan (founder of the Maihar gharaanaa), was a maestro of Surbahar. Totally absorbed in her sadhana, she stayed away from the public platform. Her genius shines through the disciples that she groomed, namely, Nikhil Banerjee, Bahadur Khan, Ashish Khan, Jotin Bhattacharya, Rajeev Taranath, Hariprasad Chaurasia, Nityanand Haldipur, Sudhir Phadke, Basant Kabra and her son, late Shubhendra Shankar.

Ansh: The first note of any moorchhana, in other words, Saa. The word was in use when the concept of the saptak (seven notes) was prevalent (see 'Saptak and Ashtak Concepts' under chapter titled 'Some Points of Controversy in Hindustani Music' for more detailed information).

Antar Gandhaar: Shuddh Gandhaar in Carnatic music terminology.

Antar mein hai to jantar mein hai: Antar here refers to what is within; Jantar is a mutation of jantra, or instrument. A saying that means 'your instrument will have what is within you'.

Antaraa: From the word antar, which means 'difference'. Refers to the second part of the khayaal composition or asthaayee. Sometimes there can be more than one antaraa in a composition. Geet, bhajan and dhrupad have several antaraas; rare khayaal compositions with more than one antaraa are also heard of (see also *Ghazal*).

Anuvaadee swara: The notes of a raga other than vaadee and samvadee (see *Vaadee, Samvaadee*).

Asardaar: Means 'effective' (from asar, meaning effect); (see also *Taaseer*).

*Ashobh raga:*Ashobh, literally, is 'hidden'. Refers to a lesser-known raga (see also *Hem-khem bhi jaantaa hai?*).

*Ashray raga:*Any raga which depends on its parental scale.

Ashtak: Octave (see chapter titled 'Some Points of Controversy in Hindustani Music' on the Ashtak for detailed comments).

Ashtepadee: Ashta means 'eight' and pada is 'verse'. Ashtapadee is the lyric form that contains eight stanzas, written by the poet Jayadev in his famous *Gita Govinda*. These ashtapadees are mostly sung in the dhrupad style and composed in dhammaar taal, roopak taal, chau taal, etc. They are also known as Havelee sangeet (see also *Havelee Sangeet*).

According to another version, ashtapadee are the works of poets, devotees of Lord Krishna. They are Ashtasakhaa or the eight friends: Soordas, Nandadas, Krishnadas, Kumbhandas, Chaturbhujdas, Parmananddas, Govindswami and Cheetswami.

Ashuddh: Literally, 'impure'. Refers to technically incorrect music.

Asihaayee: From the verb sthaa, meaning to stay. Sthaayee is the noun, meaning 'that which is stable'. Refers to the first part of the composition (see also *Mukharaa*). The 'stability' lies in the setting or fixing of the raga music to the lyric. Sometimes the word is used for the complete composition (more so by followers of the Kirana school), for it is a practice introduced by the Kirana masters (see also *Bandish, Cheez*).

Ataaee: From the word ataa, meaning 'intuition'. Used for a person who sings or plays without proper learning and guidance.

Atee Mandra: Extra low octave, lower than the mandra saptak.

Atee Taar: Very high notes higher than the saptak taar.

Atee Vilambit: Extra slow.

Avirabhaav: From avirat, meaning 'that which does not stop'. Returning to an original raga, from which a timely detour has been made into another raga (see also *Tirobhaav*). In practice, both avirabhaav and tirobhaav are terms used for the same experience, avirabhaav meaning to reappear and tirobhaav meaning to disappear.

B

Baabat: A 'definite formation' in music (when there is no vagueness at all).

Baaj: Stylistic peculiarities that are specific to the playing of instruments such as sitar, veenaa, tablaa and pakhaawaj (this does not apply to saarangee, flute or shehnaaee, for, being instruments that can play long notes, they follow the vocal manner).

Baaj kaa taar: The main string on sitar or saarangee, on which notes are produced.

Baanee: From vaach, which means 'saying'. Refers to sayings of the saints sung to music. Though now an archaic word in music, it was also used to refer to the various dialects in the language of dhrupad compositions. These baanees were: nauharee banee, daagar baanee, gandhaar or gauharee baanee, and khandahar baanee.

Baansuree: Flute. Also called venoo and muralee.

Baat ban jaanaa: To be able to establish and achieve a specific impact in a performance (see also *Jamaanaa*).

Baaul: Comes from vaatul, meaning 'frenzied'. The devotional folk form from Bengal. Bauls are a community of fakeers in Bengal who sing gaathaas (stories) from the sacred texts and the sayings of the masters—all songs of bhakti. They are often heard singing early in the morning.

Baayaan: Left piece of the tablaa pair (see also *Dhaamaa* and *Tablaa*).

Badaa khayaal: Badaa means 'large', is used to refer to vilambit (slow) khayaal, specifically the slow tempo of the khayaal (see *Vilambit*).

Badaree: Leather cord used to fix the tablaa pudee. This hard cord is made from the hide of dead animals only (see *Pudee, Tablaa*).

Bade Ghulam Ali Khan: Famous musician of the Patiala gharaanaa (1901–1968) who learnt from his uncle, Kale Khan, Ustad Bade Ghulam Ali Khan was known for his highly cultivated, sweet and melodious voice. His thumree singing was even more appreciated than his khayaal. He wrote several compositions under the pen name of Sab-rang. His disciples are Munawwar Ali Khan (his son) and Prassoon and Meera Bannerjee (of Kolkata); (see also *Patiala gharaanaa*).

Badhat: From badhanaa, meaning 'to proceed'. Refers to detailed improvisation in the aalaap (see *Behlaavaa*).

Badkhabraa: An ill-informed musician.

Bahaa huaa galaa: Bahaa huaa means 'flooded'. Refers to uncontrolled throw of the voice, where the conception and the rendering are not in coordination (in contrast with *Bahaao*).

Bahaao: Literally, 'flow'. The fluency achieved after years of practise, when for the musician there is no gap between the conception and the rendering.

Baiju Bawra: Nayak Baiju or Baijnath Mishra was the celebrated dhrupad singer and composer at the court of Raja Man Singh Tomar of Gwalior (who reigned during the years 1486–1526).

Bakar taan: Comes from the word bakraa, which means 'goat'. This taan, which sounds like the goat's bleating, refers to the unmusical taan that is lingered on by holding the breath. It has a little of the staccato effect.

Bakshu: Bakshu Nayak, famous musician of the early sixteenth century at the Gwalior darbaar (see also *Nayak*).

Benaras baaj: See *Poorab baaj.*

Bandish: Literally, 'fixed order to be observed'. Refers to the khayaal composition. It is also known as bol bandish.

Baraabar kee laya: The laya used in baraabar kee taan, which means 'two notes to one beat' (see *Baraabar kee taan*).

Baraabar kee taan: Also called doonee, in this taan two notes are applied to one beat throughout. Refers to the doubled movement of the taan worked into the beat.

Baarahmaassaa: Literally, 'twelve months', baarah meaning 'twelve', maas meaning 'month'. Folk song from Uttar Pradesh which contains references to the everyday life of the people, sung through the twelve months of the year.

Baraf: Literally, 'ice'. Musically unresponsive or emotionally frozen.

Barbat: Ancient east Asian instrument, shaped like a sarod but made of wood. Sometimes it has a few frets as well.

Barkat Ali: Younger brother of Ustad Bade Ghulam Ali Khan and great exponent of the Patiala gharaanaa, Ustad Barkat Ali remained in Pakistan after the partition of India. He sang mostly thumrees, ghazals, pahaaree, etc. His music was extremely moving. The element of Punjab ang (in thumree-daadraa) in India or Pakistan is, to this day, mostly influenced by Barkat Ali's music. Both Ghulam Ali, the popular ghazal singer of Pakistan, and Begum Akhtar have acknowledged him as their guru.

Barsee: From baras, meaning year. Barsee here means 'anniversary', which is generally observed after a musician's death.

Basnaa: Literally, 'to make oneself at home'. Refers to the point when the raga—or, as such, the performance—is established.

Bedaar, Bedaar Ang: Comes from bedor, meaning 'unsystematic' (which in turn comes from bethor, meaning baseless). Actually, bedaar ang is a phrase used in praise of the fluency of taan structures, achieved as a result of freedom from formalities of pattern.

Be-dam: Dam is 'breath'. Be-dam literally means 'non-stop'. A non-stop tukraa (piece) or tihaaee on the tablaa, falling on sam.

Been: The veenaa (see *Beenkaar* and *Veenaa*).

Beenkaar: Been is the veenaa, specifically the rudra veenaa. But beenkaar is the player of any veenaa, rudra veenaa, Saraswati veenaa or vichitra veenaa. The Beenkaar gharaanaa refers to the families in which there is the tradition of playing the rudra veenaa.

Begum Akhtar: Akhtaribai Faizabadi (1914–1974) was one of the most important exponents of the Poorab ang thumree in our times. The colour of Punjab ang mingled beautifully into her Poorab style. Begum Akhtar acknowledged Ramzan Khan (Lucknow gharaanaa), Ata Mohammad Khan, Abdul Wahid Khan (of Kirana) and Barkat Ali (Patiala) as her gurus.

Behlaavaa: Literally, 'to keep happily occupied'. To sing aalaap with bol (words from the composition); this dramatizes the specific attitude of behlaanaa.

Behr: Metre in poetry.

Belaa: Indian name for violin (a mutation of the English 'viola').

Bal: Literally, 'curves'. Refers to patterns of the taan.

Berozaa: A solid, transparent chemical used to rub the bows of the violin or saarangee to sharpen their resonance.

Besuraa: Out of tune.

Be-taal: Missing taal beats (out of rhythm); (often used when a musician is impatient and overexcited).

Bhaand: A community of entertainers or jesters who used music (partly) in their style of entertainment.

Bhaat: A community of singers whose work was to preserve the Rajput traditions of chivalry through their singing. They would sing in praise of the Rajputs and their ancestors, and inspire them to bravery in the battlefield.

Bhaav: From the verb bhoo, meaning 'to exist '(that is, 'to exist as emotion'). In dance, the noun bhaav refers to the gesture expressing a particular emotion. In music, it refers to the totality of emotional expression. There is the Sanskrit saying '*bhaavate itee bhaavaha*'—that which exists becomes bhaav; in other words emotion which exists within is expressed as bhaav.

Bhairav: From the word bhee, means 'fear', and raee, means 'sound'. Bhairav were the men and Bhairavee the women devotees of Lord Shiva, and they lived mostly in and around cremation ghaats. It is said that they exorcised the spirits of the dead. The ragas Bhairav and Bhairavee derive their names from here.

Bhajan: Any song which is devotional in mood; a bhajan can be folk-based as well.

Bhakta: Devotee (used both in the religious and musical sense).

Bharaao: From bharanaa, meaning 'to fill'. The full and heavy, rich and substantial throw of the note, as well as of the music itself.

Bharee: See *Taalee.*

Bhaskar Bua Bakhle: One of the great musicians of this century (1869–1922), Bhaskar Bua was the first Hindu to have been acknowledged as a maestro by the Muslim masters of his time.

Bhaskar Bua learnt from four ustads, two of them the well-known Ustad Nathan Khan (1840–1900) of Agra and Ustad Alladiya Khan of Jaipur. His disciples were Dilip Chandra Bedi, Master Krishna (of Prabhat Films), and Bhai Lai (who lived in Pakistan after the partition of India).

Bhatkhande: Celebrated musicologist of our time (1860–1936), who travelled extensively and collected thousands of compositions (khayaal, dhrupad, dhammaar, thumree, daadraa, tappaa and horee) from the musicians of his time and published them with notation. The gharaanaas he was able to cover were Rampur, Gwalior, Agra and Jaipur. These are available in Hindi and Marathi, in six volumes, under the name Kramik Pustakmaalikaa. Vishnu Narayan Bhatkhande also provided the ten-thaath theory to categorize Hindustani ragas, and composed several Lakshana geets and other compositions under the pen name of Chatur Pandit. He also started the famous Maurice College of Music in Lucknow.

Bhayaanak sur: Bhayaanak means 'fearful'. Refers to the 'terrifying expression' of a note.

Bhed: Literally, 'secret'. Refers to clues to musical understanding.

Bheree: A large and heavy bugle with a curved, round neck opening above and behind the head; it was in use in courts to announce the mornings and was also blown in times of war (also called dundubhee).

Bhendi Bazar gharaanaa: The first generation of the Bhendi Bazar gharaanaa includes three brothers, all of them vocalists, who came from Bijnor in the Moradabad district of Uttar Pradesh and settled in Bhendi Bazar, Mumbai. They were Chajju Khan, Nazir Khan (died1919) and Khadim Hussain Khan. Chajju Khan was a fakeer and composed several compositions under the pen name of Amar Muni. Ustad Aman Ali Khan, the son of Ustad Chajju Khan and later a major exponent of this gharaanaa, dedicated several of his own compositions to his father under the same pen name. A great number of the compositions of this gharaanaa are in praise of Lord Shiva. Anjanibai Malpekar was another well-known musician of this gharaanaa, a disciple of Ustad Nazir Khan. Shiv Kumar Shukla and Ramesh Nadkarni are the disciples of Ustad Aman Ali Khan (see also *Aman Ali Khan*).

Bhimsen Joshi: Pandit Bhimsen Joshi, great master of the Kirana gharaanaa (1922–2011), was a disciple of Sawai Gandharva. He was a legendary musician renowned for khayaal gayakee as well as devotional music (bhajans and abhangs). His style of singing drew inspiration from the great legends Kesar Bai Kerkar and Amir Khan. His students include Shrikant Deshpande, Madhav Gudi, Narayan Deshpande and Anand Bhate.

Bhurnaa: Used by musicians of the Punjab in appreciation of any fine, skilled work during rendering. This is mostly done in Bedaar ang (see *Bedaar ang*).

Bilas Khan: Famous son of Tansen, there is a well-known legend about him. At the time of Tansen's death it is said Bilas Khan sang what is now famous as Bilaaskhaanee todee, and the body of Tansen, moved by the raga, blessed him. After that, Bilas Khan was declared khaleefaa of the Tansen tradition (see *Khaleefaa*).

Bikat: A mutation of vikat, meaning 'difficult' or 'complicated' (generally used with reference to musical patterns).

Birhaa: Birhaa means 'separation'. Refers to folk songs of Uttar Pradesh in which the lyrics are about separation.

Bol: A line or phrase of the composition (asthaayee); also, a beat or a set of beats on the tablaa.

Bol aalaap: See *Behlaavaa.*

Bol baant: Baant is 'to divide'. Refers to a meaningful division of bol while singing. This is a practice prevalent in dhrupad singing or in the khayaal based on the dhrupad style.

Bol banaao: To compose phrases with bol while singing a raga, with a view to embellishment.

Bol taan: Any taan in which parts of the bol (of the composition) are knitted.

Bongaa: 'Unmusical'; idiotically out of tune and unaware of it.

Boobaas: Literally, 'smell'. Used to appreciate the 'flavour' of a particular style.

Bundu Khan: A well-known saarangee player of the Delhi gharaanaa. Disciple of Ustad Mamman Khan (who was attached to the Patiala durbaar), Bundu Khan (1886–1955) became a court musician at Indore. He played a small saarangee made of bamboo, comparatively smaller than the usual saarangee. It had a little puppet's face on its top. He was the first to change the tant into steel strings as baaj kaa taar. His son Umrao Khan was also a good saarangee player and vocalist, settled in Pakistan (see *Tant, Baaj kaa taar*).

C

Chaantee: The taut skin on the daayaan (right tablaa). The bol played on this part is called chaantee kaa bol (see *Patraa*).

Chaant-thaap: Thaap is 'stroke'. Refers to the stroke of the palm on the daayaan (the right piece of the tablaa) to get 'taa'.

Chaendaar: Chaen means 'restful'. Refers to music of a peaceful nature.

Chaitee: A type of folk song from Uttar Pradesh describing the moods of the month of Chet (March to April) in the Hindu calendar.

Chakkar: Ring or circle of taal or taan.

Chakkardaar: A series of cycles conceived in taal or taan.

Chalan: Comes from the root chaal, which means 'movement'. The word is also used to refer to custom: the practised custom or traditional manner of proceeding with a raga, observing all rules and regulations.

Chamree: Literally, 'hide'. Chamree forms a part of percussion instruments.

Chanchal or chaachar taal: See *Taal.*

Chang: A large-sized tambourine without jingles; basically a folk instrument. Also called Daph.

Chaaran: A community of bards (mostly Rajputs) who sang heroic poetry at courts, and also made announcements about the comings and goings of kings and other noblemen.

Charan: Steps in music or poetry.

Charju: A well-known musician associated with the raga Charju kee Malhaar, which contains a flavour of Desee in Malhaar.

Chatur Pandit: The pen name of Vishnu Narayan Bhatkhande (see *Bhatkhande*).

Chaturang: Chatur denotes 'four', ang means 'parts'. Refers to four musical forms or features in one composition, such as khayaal, taraanaa, taal tukraa, sargam and so on.

Chaturth jaatee: A taan which has four-note patterns or sets of squarish frames.

Chaumukhee gaayak: Chaumukhee is 'four-faced', referring to a person who can see in all directions. Refers to a musician capable of singing in any classical mode: khayaal, thumree, tappaa, taraanaa, bhajan, ghazal, etc.

Chaupaaee:A four-line couplet from the *Ramacharitmanas* by Tulsidas.

Cheez: An Urdu word, meaning 'thing' or 'gift', used to refer to the khayaal composition.

Cheez bethaanaa: Teaching of the composition to the level of perfection in the shishya or disciple (bethaanaa means 'to set in a mould').

Cheezen palatnaa or cheezen phernaa: Palatnaa or phernaa means 'to turn over'. Refers to practice during which the repertoire of compositions (or cheezen) is revised.

Chhand: The rhyme of any lyric, with accuracy of metre.

Chhaayaa lagat raga: A particular raga which has shades of other ragas. The word chab (meaning resemblance) is also used in a similar context (see *Sankeerna* and *Mishra raga*).

Chhedanaa: To play; used mostly for the taanpuraa.

Chhed-chhaad: Literally, 'to fiddle with'. To play 'this' and 'that' on an instrument, before coming into the proper mood for a performance.

Chhoot: A fast, straight taan of shooting nature, essentially skipping some notes of the scale.

Chhotaa khayaal: Drut (fast) or madhya laya (medium tempo) composition of the khayaal.

Chillaa chadhaanaa: Chillaa means 'forty'. A forty-day vow taken by a musician to practise without break or outside disturbance. The musician lives in total solitude for that period, fulfilling only the barest necessities for living. A musician can observe chillaa several times during a lifetime. The vow is taken before a peer (spiritual guru) in a dargah (shrine).

Chikaaree: The last string in a string instrument, used to improvise laya patterns.

Chinakdaaree: Chinak means 'drizzle'; also a sweet pinpricking. Refers to music charged throughout with bristling (spark-like) creativity.

Chishtee paramparaa: The Chishtee tradition. Khwaja Moinuddin Chishti Garib Nawaz (1142–1236), the Sufi saint, settled in Ajmer during the reign of Prithvi Raj Chauhan. He had many descendants; his direct disciple was Bakhtiar Kaki (died 1235), whose disciple was Sheikh Farid (1175–1265), whose disciple was Hazrat Nizamuddin Auliya (1238–1325). Amir Khusro, the celebrated poet–musician (1253–1325), was a disciple of Nizamuddin Auliya, as were several other musicians, poets and philosophers, who belonged to the Chishtee silsilaa. The musical tradition which started at that time began to be referred to as the Chishtee paramparaa. The present musical forms like khayaal, qawwaalee etc. developed within this tradition.

C.R. Vyas: Pandit C.R. Vyas (1924–2002), Hindustani classical vocalist of khayaal gaayakee, was educated at Bhatkhande Music Institute. He received training in Kirana gharaanaa under Govindrao Bhatambrekar, Gwalior gharaanaa under Rajarambua Paradkar and Agra gharaanaa under Jagannathbua Purohit. Associated with ITC for thirty-four years, he had single-minded devotion to all that is authentically traditional in Hindustani music. His disciples include Shubha Mudgal and his son Suhas Vyas.

D

Daab gaans: Daab is 'to press', gaans is 'to attain a result'. Refers to tonal weight of each bol on the tablaa.

Daab gaanth: A phrase used in praise of the heavy and rich as well as correct pressure of the hands on the tablaa.

Daad: A Persian word, meaning 'praise', especially learned praise, particularly from one master to another. The most common daad heard in the mehfil is the spontaneous 'Subhaan Allah'. Speaking highly for the artist, Subhaan Allah means 'praise be to God' (crediting Him with the achievement). Maashaa Allah, meaning 'with the blessings of God', is another popular manner of communicating daad. Others are:

- *Ghandee choomnaa:* This was a custom among vocalists of earlier times, to praise each other by kissing the part of the neck that covered the gullet.
- *Jawaab naheen:* Jawaab naheen is again a common term of praise. Jawaab is reply; to convey a sense of comparison and equality. Thus jawaab naheen means 'that which holds no comparison'. Joraa naheen is also used in the same context.
- *Lalit kee khairaat bat rahee hai:* A moving statement of praise which has almost become proverbial today. Once,

Ustad Abdul Wahid Khan (of Kirana) was performing Lalit (one of his favourite ragas) at the dargah in Ajmer Sharif. It was such a soulful rendering that the Pir Sahib said to the people, 'Lalit kee khairaat baat rahee hai'— 'Lalit is being distributed as sacrament by Wahid Khan Sahib. Please accept it.'

- *Munh mein zahar kee pudiyaa rakh kar gaanaa:* This is a proverbial expression in praise of the musician who can sing a very difficult raga, with the most sensitive phrases, with ease and flawless mastery. The expression literally means 'to sing with poison in the mouth': a little mistake and the poison would go down his throat.

- *Potaa badaa surmein hai:* A form of praise, used when a musician's fingertip work flows with maximum ease on his instrument, equalling the flight of his imagination (see also *Potaa*).

Daa-daadhaa: A mizraab stroke on the sitar by the first finger of the right hand; daa is produced by an inward stroke, and daadhaa by inward-outward strokes.

Daadar kanthee: Daadar means 'frog'; kanth is 'throat'. Refers to a musician with a loud and strained, frog-like voice.

Daadraa: A light-classical style of singing, even lighter than the thumree. Any dhun (tune) or lore is improvised in the thumree style to sing a daadraa. It is not essential that a daadraa be sung in daadraa taal—it can be in any small taal: roopak, keherwaa, khemtaa or daadraa.

Daadar means 'frog', and this light-classical form of singing gets its name from the 'jumpy and catchy' dhuns picked up from here and there for the thumree like improvisation.

Daadraa taal: See *Taal.*

Daagar: A family of dhrupad singers, originally from Jaipur (*see Daagar banee*).

Daagar baanee: One of the four dialects of the language of dhrupad compositions (see *Baanee*).

Daanedaar: Literally, 'granular'; from daanaa, meaning 'grain'. Refers to the crystal-crisp tonal quality of the notes of the taan.

Daayaan: Right piece of the tablaa.

Daggaa: Daggaa is the left piece of the tablaa, also known as baayaan, made of metal or clay.

Damroo: A large dugdugee (see *Dugdugee*).

Damkham: Dam refers to physical capacity, kham to challenge. Used for the overall capacity of any musician.

Daph: See *Chang.*

Daphlee: A small chang. This is called khanjaree in south India.

Dattatreya Puluskar: Son of Vishnu Digambar Puluskar, who died very young, at the age of thirty-four. Dattatreya Puluskar (1921–1955) had a melodious, slightly nasal voice and sang some very popular bhajans as well.

Daras Piyaa: Pen name of Ustad Mehboob Khan, a composer from the Agra gharaanaa.

Dardeelaa: From dard, meaning pain. Music creating a mood of pathos.

Dakshinaa: Daksh is to have the ability (here, to give). Refers to the sacred, ritual remuneration offered by the disciple to his guru, mostly at the end of his training, which is followed by the guru's blessing. This offer can be in the shape of a pledge, gifts or money and is marked by an attitude of deep devotion in the disciple towards his guru.

Deem tadeem: Dummy words used in taraanaa (see *Taraanaa*).

Deepchandee: See *Taal.*

Deergha swara: Deergha means 'long', or 'extended'. A prolonged note; refers specially to a vocalist's capacity for holding a long note.

Dernaa: A dummy word used in taraanaa (See *Taraanaa*).

Deshee sangeet: Hindustani music is classified under two categories: deshee and maargee. Deshee comes from desheeya, meaning regional. Community songs, folk tunes, and many classical ragas like Desee, Maand, Pahaaree, Peeloo, Barwaa, Aasaa, Sorath, Sindhuraa and Sindhraa, and Behaaree are classified under deshee sangeet (see also *Maargee sangeet*, as well as the chapter titled 'Some Common Points of Controversy in Hindustani Music.')

Deyn: Music acknowledged as a gift of God or the blessings of elders.

Dhaa: A stroke of both hands on the set of tablaas. The right hand strikes the kinaar (edge) of the tablaa to give the sound of 'Gaa'. The two strokes played simultaneously, produce 'Dhaa'.

Dhaamaa: Though now out of use, this was the left piece of the tablaa, made of wood. A round layer of dough (made from flour) was pasted flat on its centre and kept moistened while playing (see also *Baayaan* and *Daggaa*).

There is an association (of this word, dhaamaa) with a custom in north India. A ball of dough was prepared from every home to offer to Brahmins in the mornings. That special dough was dhaamme kaa pedaa and the rotee or bread prepared from it was dhaamme kee rotee. Thus the feeling of auspiciousness is associated with the word dhaamaa.

Dhaandal: 'To create a mess'. Specially used to refer to a situation in which the musician does not follow traditional principles.

Dhadhaan: An open-hand sound produced on the tablaa or pakhaawaj. Both hands strike simultaneously (see also *Ghadhaan*).

Dhaadee: Community of professional musicians from the Punjab. They also play the saarangee.

Dhaivat: Sixth note of the octave. From the root 'dhyeya', meaning 'to concentrate'. The note is produced from the point which is also the centre for concentration (or dhyaana) in the body. It is also said that dhaivat is a note understandable only to the sensitive musical ear.

Dhammaar: A dhrupad composed in dhammaar taal (see also *Dhammaar* under *Taal*).

Dhin: A bol of both hands on the set of tablaas, the right hand strikes the black centre of the daayaan, producing the sound of 'tin' and the left, striking the middle of the baayan, produces 'gaa'. Played simultaneously, they produce 'dhin'.

Dhirkit: A complete bol of four inter-bols (dhi, r, ki, t) produced by both hands on the set of tablaas. 'Dhir' is produced by the palm of the right hand.

Dhobee pataraa: The name given to a particular type of taan which could be crudely compared to the movements of a dhobee (washerman) beating clothes on a stone. A term mostly in use by the practitioners of the Delhi gharaanaa.

Dholak: A very popular percussion instrument, smaller than the pakhaawaj in its length, and equally wide on both sides. Mostly used for lighter forms like ghazal, qawwaalee, bhajan, naat and folk music. At one time even big taals were played on the dholak.

Dholnee: Women folk singers from a community in Rajasthan.

Dhrupad: Dhruv means 'unchangeable', and pada is 'lyric'. This referred, originally, only to the composed song or composition in what has today generally come to be known as the dhrupad style of singing, which includes aalaap, jor and gamak taan. This song has four parts—asthaayee (introductory part of the composition), sanchaaree (expansion of the composition which is the second part), antaraa (the third part, sung on the higher notes) and aabhog (concluding part of the composition); (see also *Baanee*).

Dillee Baaj: The stylistic tradition of tablaa which first started in Delhi. The distinctive bols of kinaar and the two fingers of the right hand are the speciality of Dillee baaj. The earliest remembered masters of this tradition are Gami Khan, his son Inam Ali, and, lately Latif Ahmad Khan.

Dilrubaa: A saarangee-like bowing instrument (see *Israaj*).

Dir dir: Dummy words used in taraanaa (see *Taraanaa*).

Dogree: A dialect spoken in the hilly areas of northern India. Several original compositions in the raga Pahaaree have been composed in this language.

Dohaa: Couplet in Hindi, Bhojpuri or Avadhi, sung to music. Known as dohraa in Punjabi. In Marathi it is dubolaa.

Doom: A community of semi-professional singers of the Punjab. The women were referred to as doomnees. They were mostly present to sing on special occasions.

Doonee: Literally, 'to double'. Used for the taan in which two notes are sung to one beat (see also *Baraabar kee taan*).

Do-taaraa: See *Ektaaraa*.

Drut: From the verb 'dru', meaning 'to move quickly or with force'. Refers to the fast composition or drut khayaal (chotaa khayaal) and drut gat (fast composition in string instruments). The word jalad, also means 'fast', is used in place of drut.

Dugdugee: A tiny drum, skinned on both sides and narrow in the middle, used mostly by street entertainers who dance monkeys.

Duggee: The left piece of the tablaa, made of clay or copper; also called baayaan or daggaa (see also *Dhaamaa*).

E

Eekaar: Vocal practise that involves singing with mouth shaped to an 'e'.

Ektaal: See *Taal.*

Ektaaraa: Ek is 'one', taaraa comes from taar or 'string'. A single-stringed folk instrument made of pumpkin and bamboo, an early version of the taanpuraa. Dotaaraa, as the name suggests, is a two-stringed instrument of the same kind. One advantage of the ektaaraa is that it serves the purpose of providing laya as well. Also known as gopiyantra.

F

Faiyaz Khan: A renowned master of the Agra gharaanaa (1886–1950), Ustad Faiyaz Khan had a heavy and melodious voice. Honoured by the title of Aaftab-e-Mausiquee (aaftaab means 'sun', mausiquee means 'music'), he was a master of both the dhrupad and khayaal forms. He also sang the thumree very well. A court musician of the Maharaja of Baroda, he wrote many compositions under the pen name of Prem Piyaa. He had several disciples: Asad Ali (who settled in Pakistan), Sohan Singh, Dilip Chandra Bedi, S.N. Ratanjankar (the musicologist) and so on (see also *Agra gharaanaa*).

Fankaar: Artist (from fan, meaning art).

Farakkabad baaj: See *Poorab baaj.*

Fikraa kehenaa: Fikraa is Urdu for sentence. Kehenaa, which means 'to say', refers in music to sing. Any swara combination can be referred to as fikraa in music.

G

Gaatree veenaa: Gaatr means 'he who sings'. Veenaa is instrument. Refers to the throat, the 'instrument' that sings.

Gaayak: Used, in general, for any vocalist.

Gaayatree: From gaee, which means 'to sing', and traee which means 'to protect'. The famous prayer or mantra from the Rig Veda, which is chanted or sung, and said to protect those who chant it.

Gaddar: Literally, 'substantial'. A substantial weightiness of the voice.

Gale mein haddee naheen: Literally, 'boneless throat'. Used in praise of a vocalist with a very flexible voice, who can render the most difficult structures with swiftness and ease.

Gamak: From the root 'gam', meaning 'to aquire pace'. Refers to a taan in which each note begins from the note preceeding it; this fills out each note with a heavier and richer tone. Gamak also means 'to warm up'.

Gandhaar: Third note of the octave. The word gandhaar is associated with gandharva desh, land of the gandharvas or celestial singers in Hindu mythology (see *Gandharva*).

Gandhaar graam: The graam 'used by the gandharvas' (for detailed explanation see Graam, and also the chapter titled 'Some Points of Controversy in Hindustani Music').

Gandharva: In Hindu mythology, the community of celestial singers; they are said to live in gandharva desh, a land in the extreme north of India (compare with 'Qandahar',) which is a province in what is today known as Afghanistan).

Gangor: The festival of Gauri poojaa, in Rajasthan (and parts of Gujarat); women pray to Goddess Gauri, the wife of Lord Shiva, to receive blessings for a happy married life. This is because the goddess was not only married to Lord Shiva, but received his love as well. The songs sung on this occasion are known as gangor-gan referring to the followers of Lord Shiva and gor to Gauri or Goddess Parvati.

Gangu Bai Hangal: Gangu Bai Hangal (1913–2009), noted exponent of Kirana gharaanaa, was a disciple of Sawai Gandharva. Gifted with a deep and powerful voice, she held sway in the field of vocal music with her rendition of khayaal gayakee over a period spanning nearly seven decades.

Garaj: Literally, 'roar'. Used in appreciation of the roaring quality of vocal throw.

Garaare: 'Gargles'. This was the commonest healing aid for the throat among vocalists of various gharaanaas. In fact, different masters were known for their particular practices (like the use of red lentil or masoor, water boiled with salt and turmeric, or ginger water, soda water, and so on).

Garmaanaa: 'To warm up'. When this refers to the warming up of the throat, it is used in appreciation. When used to refer to the performer himself, it is negative criticism, implying hot-headedness.

Gat: Comes from gatee or tempo, here meaning 'movement'. Refers to the composition played on the sitar and sarod as well as tablaa (and not the saarangee, flute or shehnaaee).

Gavaeeyaa: Professional vocalist.

Gaz: The saarangee, violin and israaj bow.

Geet: Any song which can be set to music.

Geetika: A collection of songs.

Ghaasee: Ghaasee means 'to give maximum finish'. Refers to the state when, after tremendous practise, the notes begin to sound well-cultured.

Ghadaa: Ghadaa or matkaa is the round earthernware pitcher played to keep rhythm, used in the folk music of the Punjab (see also *Ghatam*).

Ghadhaan: A resounding sound on the tablaa or pakhaawaj, played with open hands, fitted within any paran or relaa; 'dhaan' follows within a split second of 'dhaa'.

Ghadiyaal: A very large, thick brass disc hung on a frame, which booms when struck with a wooden striker.

Ghairat: The attitude of 'self-challenge' in a musician.

Ghaggaa: A hoarse-voiced musician.

Ghandee phootnaa: Ghandee is the 'pendulum' in the throat. Phootnaa is 'to break'. Used to refer to the quality of the voice in adolescence, particularly in boys.

Ghapadh chauth: Literally, 'hotch-potch', or 'jumbled'. To make a mess of a recital. Also called ghaplaa.

Ghar: Literally, 'home'. Used for any one point at the edge of the round top of the daayaan (right tablaa piece), from where the instrument is finely tuned. Ghar bandh (close ghar) and ghar khulaa (open ghar) are expressions of improper or proper tuning respectively.

Gharaanaa: A school, by style and tradition, of Hindustani music. Gharaanedaar, from gharaanaa, refers to traditional music or to a traditional musician (musician coming from a traditional music background); gharaanedaar bandish is used for a composition from a particular school reflecting a typical style (see also Agra, Gwalior, Jaipur, Bhendi bazar, Rampur, Sham Chaurasi, Kirana and Indore gharaanaas).

Ghaseet: See *Meend.*

Ghatam: Large, round earthen pitcher used to keep laya in Carnatic music (see also *Ghadaa*).

Ghazal: One of the most beautiful lyrical forms in Urdu poetry. The first couplet is known as matlaa and the concluding couplet as *maktaa.* The rest of the couplets are known as misraas (poetically) and antaraas (musically). Every couplet of the ghazal is complete by itself in its expression or mood or message.

Ghudaj: The bridge on the sitar, taanpuraa and veenaa. This is made of stag horn, camel bone or ivory (a brass bridge, however, is used on the Saraswati veenaa).

Gidda: The folk dance of the Punjab, involving two or three girls who clap each others' hands while dancing and singing.

Ginatkaar: Master of taal, not essentially of laya (see *Layakaar*).

Girah lagaanaa: Literally, 'to knit a knot'. Refers to some additional bols of content similar to the mukhraa, sung in the qawwaalee, bhajan and daadra (see *Mukhadaa*).

Girija Devi: Girija Devi (1929–2017) was a renowned classical vocalist of the Seniya and Banaras gharaanaas. Her mentors were Pandit Sarju Prasad and Pandit Shrichandra Misra. She was master of both Hindustani classical and light classical music. She performed the purab ang of the Banaras gharaanaa. She sang khayaal, thumree, daadra and tappa. Her repertoire in light classical music included Kajri, Chaiti and Hori. Dalia Rahut, Jayita Pande and Satya Narayan Misra are some of Girija Devi's prominent disciples.

Gokulotsavji Maharaj: One of the most accomplished Hindustani classical vocalists of khayaal and dhrupad gayan of this generation, Gokulotsavji Maharaj is an exponent of the Indore gharaanaa tradition and a master of haveli sangeet. He has created several new raagas and innumerable compositions in Sanskrit, Persian, Urdu and Braj Bhasha.

Gopal Nayak: A leading musician, contemporary of Amir Khusro at the court of Allauddin Khilji, Gopal Nayak had a large number of followers and disciples. He was so highly respected by them that they used to carry him on their shoulders in a paalkee (palanquin).

Graam: Literally, 'township'. Refers essentially to the area or 'township' of the saptak according to the earlier system. There were three graams, shadaj madhyam graam and gandhaar graam. Shadaj graam referred to the fixing of Saa on the fourth shrutee while arranging the twenty-two shrutees in the order of 4-3-2, 4-4-3-2. Madhyam or the actual middle note falls on the middle four. Madhyam graam refers to the fixing of shadaj on Maa.

Graam is not to be confused with scale, as the concept of seven notes belongs to the time before Iranian and Portuguese influence on Indian music. A third graam, gandhaar graam, is known to 'exist in heaven' according to Hindu mythology (in fact, it is known to have been 'lost' to the heavens) (see also chapter titled 'Some Points of Controversy in Hindustani Music' for an elaborate explanation of Gandhaar graam).

Graha swara: Home note or starting note of the raga, graha swara refers to any note of the octave which is conceived as a base to proceed futher into another raga. Ultimately this note becomes Saa (see also *Moorchhana*). In the shastras, graha refers to planet (or the planetary system governing our lives). Thus graha swara in the raga is its governing note as well.

Granthee: The person who narrates the Guru Granth Sahib in the gurudwaaraa.

Gul: Persian word, meaning flower. Refers to one of the stylistic features of the quwwaalee which is almost out of practice today.

Gulukaaraa: Female vocalist (see also *Mughanneeyaa*).

Gunee: From guna, which means 'quality'. Used to refer to a highly respected and knowledgeable musician.

Guroo (also Guru): From gu, meaning 'ignorance', and roo, meaning 'to remove' or 'destroy'. Refers to the preceptor who shows the life-path (see also *Shishya*).

Guru-bhaaee, guru-behen: Disciples of the same guru are known as guru-bhaee, or guru-behen. Traditionally these relationships have been no less important than real sibling relationships.

Gurudakshinaa: See *Dakshinaa*.

Guru Poornimaa: Guru Poornimaa or Vyas poojaa is the day for guru poojaa. Guru Vyas Dev, son of Parashar Muni, bore the name of Krishnadweepaayan, meaning 'the dark one, born on an island'. He is the author of the Mahabharata, and therefore the aadee guru or the first guru. Guru poojaa is also therefore known as Vyas poojaa; and the guru's seat is often called Vyas gaddee. Poomima, or the night of the full moon (poorna meaning 'full' and ima meaning 'to move') falls every month; guru poornimaa falls on the full moon day of the month of Aashaadh according to the Hindu calendar.

Guru-shishya paramparaa: Paramparaa can be broken into para meaning 'other', and 'paraha', meaning 'chain', or 'link'. Paramparaa, therefore, is 'tradition', here the master–disciple tradition, which has provided the only base for the preservation of the classical arts (see also *Guru* and *Shishya*).

Gurmukh vidyaa: Literally, 'knowledge' from the mouth of the guru. Refers to the oral tradition—to learn from the guru, sitting at his feet.

Guththam-guththaa: Jumbling of the patterns of the taan (see also *Ladant*).

Gwalior gharaanaa: One of the oldest gharaanaas of khayaal singing, the stylistic features of the Gwalior gharaanaa are: the use of medium laya even in badaa khayaal, and skilful taan, bol-taan and bol-banth. Many other gharaanaas are considered offshoots of this gharaanaa, like the Patiala, Rampur and the Vishnu Digambar schools.

The gharaanaa traces its ancestry to Nathan Peerbaksh, to the two sons of Bade Mohammad Khan—Haddu and Hassu Khan—Bade Nissaar Hussain, Rehmat Khan Bawle (died 1922), Balkrishna Bua Ichalkaranjikar (1849–1926), Vishnu Digambar, Shankar Rao (1863–1917), Krishnarao Shankar Pandit, Rajabhaiya Poonchwale, and so on. L.K. Pandit continues the tradition.

Kumar Gandharva (died 1992) was one of the finest interpreters of the Gwalior gharaanaa. He gave to the world of Hindustani music several good compositions and a few new ragas, out of which Malawatee is the most memorable.

H

Haafiz Ali Khan: Renowned sarodiyaa of the Gwalior durbaar (1888–1972). He learnt from Ganpatrao Bhaiya Saheb of Gwalior, and from Chukhalalji and Ganeshilalji of Brindavan, and from Wazir Khan of Rampur, who was also the guru of Ustad Allauddin Khan of Maihar, among others; Hafiz Ali Khan has left behind his son and prime disciple Amjad Ali Khan.

Haahaakaar: Used jocularly for over-broad aakaars, producing a hollow, noisy effect (the term was introduced by Ustad Amir Khan).

Haano: Used for the hollowness of a musician.

Hak adaa karnaa: To do justice to the raga, style, etc.

Halak taan: Halak means 'throat'. Refers to the deep-throated taan, with gamak, producing a rich effect (see also *Taan*).

Halak bol: Bol rendered full-throatedly.

Harasva swara: Haarasva means 'short'. A note of short duration (see also *Deergha swara*).

Harballabh: Baba Harballabh was a music-loving fakeer of the late nineteenth century who lived in east Punjab. A music festival is held in his memory every year from 26–29 December, and is one of the oldest festivals of north India. It began more than a century ago at his samaadhee at Devi Talao, Jalandhar.

Haridas Swami: The famous saint–musician of the Gosain paramparaa. He was born in Multan in 1537. A devotee of Lord Krishna, Swami Haridas (died 1632), migrated to Vrindaban. He had eight famous disciples, one of them being Tansen, famous musician at Akbar's court (1556–1605), and, it is said, Nayak Baijnath (or Baiju Bawra) (however, this is a well-known controversy, for Baiju Bawra has been heard of at the court of Raja Man Singh Tomar at Gwalior as well). Haridas Jayanti is celebrated at Vrindaban every year at his samaadhee.

Hari Prasad Chaurasia: Pandit Hari Prasad Chaurasia (born 1938) is a renowned flautist in the Hindustani classical tradition. He started learning vocal music from Rajaram, but later, switched to playing the flute under the tutelage of Bholanath Prasanna of Varanasi. He also trained extensively under Annapurna Devi. Apart from classical music, Pandit Hari Prasad Chaurasia has had a rich collaboration with Indian and Western musicians. Prominent among his disciples are Pashupatinath Arya, Debopriya and Suchismita, and his nephew, Rakesh Chaurasia.

Harkat: A small movement of notes.

Harmonium: This is the organ-like instrument commonly used in all kinds of music in India (especially in the north). Its tuning is based on the tempered scale.

Har Rang: Pen name of an eighteenth-century composer.

Hathelee kaa bol: Hathelee is palm. Term used for dhirkit on the tablaa, in which the palm of the right hand is used along with the left (see *Dhirkit*).

Havelee sangeet: Bhakti songs from the Vishnu sampradaaya, particularly the poet Jayadev's ashtapadees, as well as ashtapadees of the Ashtasakhaas sung in dhrupad style and also known as havelee dhrupad. Havelees were old mansions where this music was sung (see also *Ashtapadee*).

Heerabai Barodekar: Disciple of Ustad Abdul Karim Khan Saheb and Ustad Abdul Wahid Khan Saheb, Heerabai was a veteran representative of the Kirana gaayakee.

Hem-khem bhi jaanta hai?: The term leads to an enquiry about a musician's knowledge and practice about rare ragas. Hem Kalyaan and Khem Kalyaan are two varieties of Kalyaan mixtures which are rarely sung. Moreover, the difference between Hem and Khem is so minute and delicate that it is really a master's job to keep the distinction while rendering. Hem is a compound of Kamod and Shuddh Kalyaan whereas Khem Kalyaan is a compound of Kamod and Eman Kalyaan.

Hindustaani raga: Ragas from the Hindustani system of music, as opposed to the Carnatic, are generally equal in the first half (poorvaang) and second half (uttaraang) in the scale of the raga.

In Hindustani music the raga is more than a scale. Each note has its own character, a certain note is emphasized, another is reluctantly used, another is used in a swinging manner, and so on and so forth. Furthermore, there is a question-answer element in the raga based on the equal situation of the notes. Finally, there is the pakar or grip (see *Pakar*). These regulations for Hindustani ragas are applicable for all basic ragas and not for mishra or sankeerna ragas (see *Mishra raga, Sankeerna raga*). For, rarely, there is an exception to this rule, as in the case of Maarwah and Vibhaas.

Hissaa: Literally, 'part'. Used in praise of a musician who specializes in any aspect of music.

Hoonkaar: Vocal practise that involves singing with mouth closed to a humming sound, also producing the nasal sound of 'hoon' (see also *Aakaar, Eekaar, Okaar*).

Horee: A form of thumree in the raga Kaafee in which the lyric is always about Holi (the festival of colours). This is sung during the months of February and March. Horee dhammaar is dhammaar in which the lyric is about Holi. Horee kaafee is used in the same sense as horee.

I

Inayat Khan: The son of Imdad Khan, he was one of the finest sitar players of his time (1894–1938). Court musician at Gauripur (Bengal), he was extremely tuneful. His sons are Vilayat Khan and Imrat Khan.

Indore gharaanaa: The gharaanaa traces its ancestry to Chhange Khan, his son Shahmir Khan, whose son was the famous Ustad Amir Khan. Basically from Kalanaur in what is known as Haryana today, Shahmir Khan settled in Indore. This gharaanaa was greatly influenced by the Bhendi Bazar and Kirana gharaanaas. Shahmir Khan became a disciple of the Bhendi Bazar musicians to understand the Merukhand system. Amir Khan, who received this Merukhand taaleem through his father, also greatly admired Ustad Abdul Wahid Khan of Kirana and Ustad Rajab Ali Khan of Devas. Thus the style became very rich and today is considered to have influenced a major cross-section of the musician and student community in Hindustani music.

The stylistic features of this gharaanaa are: detailed bardat (aalaap) with bol in vilambit laya based on Merukhand thinking, emphasis on cultivation of mandra and madhya saptak because of detailed badhat; a suggestive awareness of laya even in vilambit; playful use of complicated sargam and rich structural improvisation in taan (also, at times, based on Merukhand). Later musicians of this gharaanaa included Amarnath, Srikant Bhakre, Singh Bandhu, Poorbi Mukherjee and Gokulutsavji Maharaj.

Israaj: Hindi name of the saarangee-like bowing instrument which has fixed frets (pardaas) like the sitar. Also known as taaoos in Persian and dilrubaa in Urdu (see also *Pardaa, Taaoos* and *Dilrubaa*).

Itr: Literally, 'essence'. Used for example as itr gaanaa-bajaanaa, which means 'to sing' or play the essentials of the raga aesthetically.

J

Jaandaar: Literally, 'powerful'. Refers to substantial weight in note, taan and overall musical projection, with regard to both vocalist and instrumentalist.

Jaatee: The classification of a raga by the number of notes used therein. The minimum notes for the raga are five; it is then known as odav raga. Six is referred to as shaadav, and seven to sampoorna. If the aarohee has five notes and the avrohee seven, the raga would be referred to as odav-sampoorna; if the aarohee is of six notes and the avrohee of seven, it would be shaadav-sampoorna, and so on.

Jabraa; jabredaar: Jabraa is 'jaw'. Jabredaar refers to the 'use of the jaw in vocalization'. This is predominant in certain styles. However, the use of the jaw in singing meets with strong disapproval by musicians of other gharaanaas, who feel it is a major defect in the throw of the voice, especially in the gamak or taan.

Jagah: Literally, 'place'. While exploring the raga, any specific phrase, big or small, is called jagah. Used often for any special or difficult piece in music.

Jaipur gharaanaa: Also known as the Atrauli or Kohlapur gharaanaa. Jaipur begins its major articulation with Ustad Alladiya

Khan. The stylistic features of this gharaanaa are raga expansion in moderate tempo; use of obvious laya throughout and simple and repetitive taan patterns sung with sustained breath in open aakaar. The musicians of this gharaanaa (immediately following Ustad Alladiya Khan) were his two sons, Munji Khan (who died in 1937) and Bhurji Khan (who died in 1950), Bhaskar Rao Bakhle, Bhai Lai (father of Bhai Chagan), Kesarbai Kerkar, Mogubai Kurdgekar, Govindrao Tembe (1881–1955), Master Krishna Dilip Chandra Bedi, and Mallikarjun Mansur, with Nivritti Bua Sarnaik and Kishori Amonkar being the major later vocalists of the gharaanaa.

Mallikarjun Mansur (died 1992) was one of the shining stars of the Jaipur gharaanaa. Till his last he was very staunch in his style, singing with a strong sense of adherence to the gharaanaa gayakee.

Dilip Chandra Bedi belonged to both the Jaipur and Agra gharaanaas, having learnt from Bhaskar Bua Bakhle, and later becoming a disciple of Ustad Faiyaz Khan; yet he developed his own style, with a Punjab flavour. A Sikh orphan from the Chabhal district of Amritsar, he was adopted by Bhaskar Bua. He died in 1993 at the age of ninety-five.

Jaltarang: Jal means 'water' and tarang means 'waves'. This instrument consists of China cups of various sizes filled with different quantities of water, with which they are tuned. The cups are arranged in a semi-circle, one to one-and-a-half feet in length, to be played and struck with a pair of bamboo sticks. This instrument is naturally conducive for moderate or fast gat.

Jamaanaa: To establish the impact of one's music without having resorted to gimmickry. The success of this depends mostly on the state of mind of the musician (see also *Baat ban jaanaa*).

Janak raga: The parental raga (janak is father) Janya raga is the raga derived from Janak raga (see *Aadee raga, Upraga*).

Jasraj: Great master of the Mewati gharaanaa, Pandit Jasraj was born in 1930. His gurus were his father, Moti Ram, his brother, Maniram, Ghulam Kader Khan of the Mewati gharaanaa, Swami Vallabhdas of the Agra gharaanaa and Raja Jaywant Singh Waghel, ruler of Saanand state who was also his spiritual guru. His disciples include Saptarshi Chakraborthy, Sanjeev Abhyankar, Kala Ramnath, Tripti Mukherjee, Suman Ghosh, Shashank Subramanyam, Kavita Krishnamurthy, Anuradha Paudwal, Sadhana Sargam, Shankar Mahadevan and Ramesh Narayan.

Jattaal: See *Taal.*

Javaa: A V-shaped piece of hard string inserted into the forefinger by the sarodiyaa for striking his instrument. The part that is held is filled with soft thread or wax, or both, for the grip.

Jawaaree: Point of resonance on the bridge of the taanpuraa, sitar or veenaa. Associated with the word is jawaahar, which in Urdu is often used to describe the shine of a gem or a pearl. When moving the thread on the taanpuraa to a certain point, it resounds with a bright resonance.

Jazbaat: Emotion in music.

Jhanj: A brass instrument consisting of a pair of hat-shaped plates which are struck together to produce a dramatic clang.

Jhaalaa: Jod on faster laya, in which chikaaree (the last string of the sitar or sarod) is included to form a variety of laya patterns.

Jhaalaa swara: Used to denote a pitch lower than the normal capacity of an instrument or the voice.

Jhampaa: See *Taal.*

Jhampak: See *Taal.*

Jhoomraa: See *Taal.*

Jhankaar: The collective strain of different musical sounds.

Jhaptaal: See *Taal.*

Jhoothaa kare to sachchaa hoye, sachchaa kare to birlaa: This is a saying which means that if a musician is ill-informed but is practising seriously, he can become true, and if a true musician is practising with ardour, he becomes a rare being.

Jitendra Abhisheki: Pandit Jitendra Abhisheki (1929–1998) was a distinguished vocalist, composer and scholar of Hindustani classical, semi-classical and devotional music. He is also credited with the revival of Marathi musical theatre in the 1960s. Besides his son Shounak Abhisheki, his well-known disciples include Asha Khadilkar, Devaki Pandit, Shubha Mudgal, Ajit Kadkade, Raja Kale, Prabhakar Karekar, Vijay Koparkar, Mahesh Kale, Sameer Dublay and Dr Hrishikesh Majumdar.

Jod: To improvise the raga highlighting the laya, not essentially the taal. In other words, a laya-oriented piece. This form of improvisation is more suitable for string instruments, as well as for dhrupad-dhammaar. Jod aalaap is almost the same as jod, but in an even slower tempo.

Jodaa: The two middle strings of the taanpuraa tuned to the basic shadaj (Saa).

Jod-jhaalaa: Jod and jhaalaa, sometimes referred to together.

Jugalbandee: A performance of two instrumentalists or vocalists (see also *Sawaal-jawaab*).

K

Kaafeeaa: Rhyming verse, sung in qawwaalee or ghazal.

Kaaklee nishaad: Shuddha nishaad in Carnatic music. This note is slightly higher than the Shuddha nishaad of Hindustani music; because of this note the Teevra Maa in Carnatic music is also higher than the Teevra Maa of Hindustani music.

Kaansen: A mutation of the word Tansen, this word (from kaan, meaning ear), originally referred to those who could not become musicians but succeeded in becoming good listeners. Often used to refer to products of music schools which produced listeners but not virtuosi. The word (with its undertone of satire) was introduced by Vishnu Digambar Puluskar.

Kaashtarang: Indian name for the xylophone or vibrophone. The word break-up here is kaasht meaning 'wood', and tarang, meaning 'waves' (tarang is made up of tri, meaning 'to cross', and gam meaning 'movements').

Kabir: A legendary saint–poet (born 1398) who lived in Benaras. He wrote hundreds of devotional songs which became very popular among the common folk of north India. Some of the versions of his sayings, known as Kabeer saakhee, have been used abundantly in both folk and classical singing (see also *Nirgun*).

Kadar Baksh: A famous tablaa ustad of Punjab, who died in Pakistan a little before the Partition. The well-known Alla Rakha, and the late Bahadur Singh (also of Punjab) are among his disciples.

Kadaan: The simultaneous strokes on both pieces of the tablaa with open hands, giving a booming bol.

Keherwaa: See *Taal.*

Kajaree: Comes from kajraa, meaning black mascara for the eyes. A folk form of Uttar Pradesh, containing songs related to the rains.

Kalaa: The word can be broken into ka meaning beautiful, and la referring to laya. Kalaa is a broad term referring to any art.

Kana: Literally, 'a small part of the khatkaa' (see *Khatkaa*).

Kanjar: A community to which singing and dancing girls known as kanjaree belonged. Today this word is a term of abuse.

Kanraseeaa: A good listener of music (kaan means 'ear', raseeaa comes from rasa, meaning 'pleasure').

Kanthe Maharaj: A very good tablaa player of Benaras, born in 1880. His disciples are Kishan Maharaj and Godai Maharaj (Samta Prasad).

Kapat taan: Kapat means 'to deceive'. The term is used for a deceptive attitude in taan, in what is apparent as taan but is sorely defective in terms of the raga, or lacks tonal qualities.

Karakht: Harsh throw of the voice. Also known as karkash.

Kartaal or Khadtaal: Kar means 'hand'. Kartaal is a wooden pair of cymbals held in the hand to keep taal, and used mostly for bhajans or in folk music. One cymbal is held by the thumb and the second by three or four of the other fingers, and struck together. The pairs are of different sizes.

Kasbal: Kasbal means 'strength' or 'capacity'. The word is used when a musician is in great form and able to excute successfully with full force (or bal) the taans that he conceives in his mind.

Kathik: Comes from kathaa, which means 'storytelling'. These were a class of musicians who narrated Pauranic stories in bhaav and in singsong style at the courts; later they evolved a dance style of their own which came to be known as Kathak. Laya and footwork are highlights of the Kathak style.

Katt: A bol of the right hand on the centre of the tablaa in which the four fingers, closed together, are sounded at one go.

Kavitt: An epic poem sung to local and regional tunes.

Keertan: From the word keertee; means 'praise to the Lord'. A form of devotional singing in which the devotees join in with the main singers, mostly during the refrain or tek. Instruments like ektaaraa, khol, manjeeraa and kartaal are used in keertan. Keertans were popularized in the sixteenth century by Chaitanya

Mahaprabhu (1485–1533) in Bengal. The person leading the keertan is the keertankaar.

Kesarbai Kerkar: Celebrated musician of the Jaipur school (1892–1977), Kesarbai was one of the foremost disciples of Ustad Alladiya Khan. She had a powerful voice and was admired for her sustained breath and pleasing personality. She was a staunch follower of the Jaipur gaayakee. Rabindranath Tagore gave her the name 'Surashree'.

Keshkee nishaad: Komal nishaad in Carnatic music (see also *Kaaklee nishaad*).

Khaalee: The first beat of the khand, other than taalee, in the taal cycle. The principle behind khaalee and taalee is to divide the taal into comprehensible frames and identify the progress of the taal.

Khaanaa pooree: Khaanaa pooree literally means 'filling up space'. It is sometimes used in ragas for a dummy note to keep the balance of the 'other half'—for example, Shivmat Bhairav is a compound of Todee and Bhairav. The addition in Bhairav of Komal gaandhaar is understood to be an additional note for Todee. But to compensate this additional note for Todee, in the second half Komal nishaad has nothing to do with Todee or Bhairav.

Now take Maaru Bihag. Although the raga sounds complete with Teevra madhyam only, Shuddh madhyam is also used in the raga to complete the other samvaads.

Khan Saheb: Khan means 'badshah' or King in the Afghan dialects. Respectfully used as a form of address for a Muslim musician.

Khaleefaa: Khaleefaa means 'chief' or 'head'. In the guru–shishya paramparaa, the son of a deceased guru, traditionally, is declared khaleefaa (see *Guru bhaaee*).

Khamsaa: The word means 'containing five' in Persian. Refers to any devotional song which extends to five couplets; a form of qawwaalee.

Khand: Khand means 'portion' or 'part'. Used to refer to the taal chambers. For instance, teentaal, consisting of sixteen beats (maatras) is divided into four chambers of four beats each. Any further distinction in the taal, for instance khaalee or taalee, is based on the first beat of any khand.

Khanjaree: Very much like a chang or daph, but of smaller size (see *Chang*).

Kharaj bharna: Term used for vocal stay at the lowest Saa, using the full breath. Kharaj helps to steady the throw of the voice. The duration for this practice varies according to the quality of the voice and the style of singing (see also *Mandra Saadhanaa*).

Kharhar Priyaa: Kaafee thaath, with Gaa nee komal, in Carnatic music is Kharhar Priyaa Mela (see also *Mela*).

Khatkaa: Quickly shaken notes in a musical phrase (see also *Kana*).

Khayaal: Since the sixteenth century, khayaal has emerged as the most popular classical form of singing in Hindustani music. In Persian and Urdu, khayaal means 'imagination'; however, the form is of purely Indian origin. It has tremendous scope and the capacity to absorb various features of musical expression such as aalaap, sargam, bol, bol-taan, behlaavaa, badhat, gamak, khatkaa, murkee, phandaa, asthaayee, antaraa and so on. These features existed in earlier forms of music, for example dhrupad, prabandha, jaatee, saadhaaranee (as mentioned in the Sangeet Ratnaakara).

Originally, khayaal was poetry composed in raga (the expression of imagination in poetry). Gradually it developed into a musical form wider in concept. Khayaal also means dhyaana or 'concentration', which is a musical requirement in rendering.

Khayaal gaayakee: The distinctive attitude of khayaal rendering in general is known as khayaal gaayakee. This is to be differentiated from gharaanaa gaayakee, in that it contains the basic principles of the khayaal, which are not necessarily stylistic.

Khemtaa: See *Taal.*

Khol: A mridang-shaped percussion instrument, made of clay. It is narrower on the right side. Used in devotional folk music, especially bhajan, and the keertan of Bengal.

Kinaar: Kinaar is the edge of the right-hand tablaa which produces the sound of Naa or Taa.

Kinnar, Kinnaree: In Hindu mythology, the community of celestial instrumentalists, instrumentalists of the gods or the accompanists of gandharvas or celestial singer-musicians (who also sang for the gods). Kinnar were male and kinnaree veenaa is the instrument played by the kinnars.

Kirana gharaanaa: This gharaanaa takes its name from Kirana, a small town near Saharanpur, Uttar Pradesh. The special feature of the gaayakee is its badhat or detailed improvisation of the raga. The renowned artists of this gharaanaa were Abdul Wahid Khan, Abdul Karim Khan and Sawai Gandharva (for more details see *Abdul Wahid Khan, Abdul Karim Khan* and *Sawai Gandharva*).

Kishan Maharaj: Pandit Kishan Maharaj (1923–2008), outstanding tablaa maestro, hailed from a lineage of Hindustani classical music tradition from Banaras. Widely travelled at home and abroad, and a recipient of several prestigious awards, he received his training from his father, Hari Maharaj, and uncle, Kanthe Maharaj. His disciples include Sukhvinder Singh Namdhari, Balkrishna Iyer and Ranesh Mishra.

Kishori Amonkar: Kishori Amonkar (1932–2017) was one of the foremost vocalists in the khayaal gayakee tradition of the Jaipur-Atrauli gharaanaa of Hindustani classical music. Groomed by her mother Mogubai Kurdikar, she was an innovative exponent of this gharaanaa whose personal style reflected the influence of other gharaanaas. She also performed thumris in the Light classical genre and devotional songs or bhajans. Apart from being a renowned musician, Kishori Amonkar was noted for her lectures on the theory of 'Rasa' in music. Her disciples include Manik Bhide, Meena Joshi, Suhasini Mulgaonkar, Arun Dravid, Raghunandan Panshikar, Arati Ankalikar, Devaki Pandit, Meera Panshikar, Shivraj Shitole, Nandini Badekar and her granddaughter Tejashree Amonkar.

Kitt: A bol of both hands on the tablaa, ki is played flat by the full palm on the left, and then t follows with the three last fingers of the right hand on the right piece of the tablaa.

Kitt-tak: A bol, consisting of the syllables ki, t, t, k played with both hands on the tablaa. Ki is played by the palm of the left hand, then 't' on the same tablaa twice, by the right forefinger, and finally, k, once again in the manner of the first, that is ki.

Kokil kanth: Kokilaa is the 'nightingle'. Kanth is 'throat'. Means 'sweet-voiced', like the nightingale.

Komal: Literally, 'soft'. Used for the minor notes of the scale.

Koodha: From koodaa, which means 'rubbish'. A person with a false understanding of music.

Koot taan: A term used generally for any complicated taan (the word koot comes from kotee, meaning 'countless').

Kram: Literally, 'order'. Refers to any pattern in swara or laya which can be continued.

Kriti: From kri meaning 'fulfilment', and tin meaning 'him who does'. The word means 'creation'. Used in Carnatic music for a complete composition in a raga, including taanam, etc.

Pandit Kumar Gandharva: Pandit Kumar Gandharva, originally known as Shivputra Siddharamayya Komkalinath (1924–1992), was a Hindustani classical vocalist who began his training with B.R. Deodhar at age eleven. His quick mastery of technique and musical knowledge was remarkable. Known for his unique vocal style he was free of the tradition of any gharaanaa. Stricken with tuberculosis for a long time, he recovered and continued singing. His innovative approach towards music led to the creation of new ragas.

Kuwaad: Comes from aadha, meaning 'off-the-beat' laya. Refers to consciously out-of-beat (in fact odd), and again out-of-beat of the out-of-beat (odd of odd) laya.

L

Laasya: In Indian mythology, the dance created by Goddess Parvati, in which emotions of love are depicted.

Lachchaa shaakh: Literally, 'bunches' on a branch. Refers to a composition containing six ragas.

Ladant: Literally, 'a fight'. Musical patterns rendered in reciprocating challenge.

Ladee: Literally, 'string' containing repetitive units. Used to describe the continuity of any musical pattern.

Lagaao: Literally, 'application'. Refers to the manner in which the throw of the voice has been cultivated (see *Swara saadhanaa* under *Saadhanaa*).

Laggee: The recurring increase in tempo and simultaneous improvisation by the tablaa in the rendering of ghazal, daadraa and thumree.

Laghoo maatraa: Laghoo means 'small'; used for the half beat, this maatra is mostly employed in notation.

Lagojaa: The double flute, a folk instrument of Punjab.

Lahajaa: Accent—not of words but of the music.

Lahak: A softly rendered gamak (see *Gamak*).

Laharaa: A fixed musical piece, set to any raga, or taal, played repeatedly on the saarangee or harmonium to keep the metre for a tablaa or pakhaawaj solo.

Lakkar aawaaz: Lakkar is wood. Refers to lack of pliability in the voice.

Langar: Literally, 'a ship's anchor'. Used to refer to the stabilization of a musical performance.

Lapetdaar: Lapet refers to anything 'wound up'. A taan structure which repeatedly winds back the alankaars.

Larzaa: The tiniest particles of sound texture, easily identifiable in the lowest notes.

Laut palat: Laut is to 'come back'. Palat is to 'repeat'. A taan which comes back and then turns in the same manner.

Laxman Krishna Rao Pandit: Pandit Laxman Krishnarao Pandit (born 1934) is fifth in an unbroken lineage of legendary musicians of Gwalior gharaanaa. Groomed by his father, Pandit Krishnarao Shankar Pandit in khayaal, tappa, taraana, ashtapadi and thumree, he has distinguished himself as exponent and guru with great command on ashtaang gayakee comprising alap-behlawa, bol-alaap, taan, bol-taans, layakari, gamak, meend-soot, and murki-khatka-jamjama. His repertoire contains rare, ancient bandishes.

Laya: Literally means 'to merge'. Refers to tempo, the continuity of beats (maatra) with equal intervals. Layadaaree is the perfection of laya as well as taal. Medium tempo is referred to as madhya laya and fast tempo as drut laya (there is also a phrase, 'maran laya': maran meaning 'the process of dying'; this refers to a 'deadly slow' tempo).

Layakaar: Master of laya, not necessarily of taal (see *Ginatkaar*).

Lebhaggoo: A person who does not learn music but picks it up from here and there.

Lop hogayaa: Lop means 'hidden'. Used to refer to a raga that is lost in history; sometimes, it is used to refer to a note that is somehow felt but is not used in a raga.

Lucknow baaj: See under *Poorab baaj*.

M

Maaheeyaa: Literally, 'the lover'. Here the word refers to romantic folklore from the Punjab.

Maand: A folk dhun from Rajasthan; as a raga it is categorized under deshee ragas. Aasaa of Punjab is mostly similar to Maand (see chapter titled 'Some Points of Controversy in Hindustani Music').

Maargee Sangeet: Music based on a particular system, referring here to raga-based music. The word maargee has come from mrg, which in Sanskrit means 'to search for' (that is, a path). This is the root for maarg, meaning 'path'. Therefore, classical music, which is the result of search, finds out specific paths, that is, ragas. This does not apply to regional ragas, like Des, Maand, Pahaaree, Sindhee, as they belong to Deshee Sangeet (see chapter titled 'Some Points of Controversy in Hindustani Music' for detailed explanation). There is the beautiful Sanskrit saying, *'mrigyate itee maargaha '*, which means 'to search is the path'.

Maatra: The beating of laya.

Madhyam: Central note of the saptak (or seven notes). The ancient Indian system of twenty-two shrutees is divided into seven swaras as 4, 3, 2, 4, 4, 3, 2—the 4 at the centre, or the 13th shrutee, is madhyam, meaning 'centre'. But even after the ashtak (octave) has come into practice, the same shrutee, or the fourth note, still bears the same name (see also chapter titled 'Some Points of Controversy in Hindustani Music' for detailed explanation).

Makrand Pandey: Tansen's Hindu name. According to Acharya Brihaspati, a contemporary historian, this was the name of Tansen's father (see *Tansen*).

Maktaa: The last couplet of the ghazal (see *Matlaa, Ghazal*).

Malini Rajurkar: Malini Rajurkar (born 1941) is a noted Hindustani classical vocalist of the Gwalior gharaanaa. She is a master of Khayaal and Tappa gayakee who was groomed under the tutelage of Govindrao Rajurkar and Vasant Rajurkar.

Mallikarjun Mansoor: Pandit Mallikarjun Mansoor (1910–1992) was a great master of the Khayaal style in the Jaipur-Atrauli gharaanaa. Trained initially in Carnatic music by Appaya Swamy, he was introduced to Hindustani music under Nilkanth Bua Alurmath of Miraj who belonged to the Gwalior gharaanaa. He then studied with Manji Khan, later with Bhurji Khan, and after the latter's death, with his son, Azizuddin Khan. Well known for his command over a large number of rare (aprachalit) ragas, he gradually evolved his own style of rendition.

Manarang: Famous khayaal composer of the Gwalior gharaanaa, whose real name was Bhupat Khan. It is said that he was the son of Sadarang, and lived during the eighteenth century (the reign of Mohammed Shah, 1719–1748).

Mand gatee: Slow movement (mand means 'slow', and gatee means 'movement').

Mandal or maadal: A tribal drum used in folk music.

Mandra: The lower octave, or the lowest notes, the range varying from musician to musician (mandra saadhanaa is the term used for practising singing in the lower octaves); (see also *Kharaj bharna*).

Mangal gaan: Mangal is auspicious. Songs for auspicious occasions.

Mani Prasad: Pandit Mani Prasad (born 1930) is a renowned musician of Kirana gharaanaa. His gurus were his grandfather, Pandit Shakti Lal, father, Pandit Sukhdev Prasad, and uncles, Pandit Shankar Lal and Pandit Gopal Prasad. His disciples include Ranjitsinh Pratapsinh Gaekwad of Baroda, Savita Devi, Rita Ganguly, Ramesh Jule, Pandit Vishwanath, Uma Garg, Surinder Kaur and Chandan Das.

Manjeera: A pair of small saucer-shaped brass cymbals used for keeping rhythm during the rendering of bhajans in folk music.

Manjula rasanaa: Manjula means 'sweet'; rasanaa means 'vaanee' or 'speech'. One of the names of Saraswati, the goddess of art and learning.

Mantra: From manan, which means 'constant' thinking or repetition in the mind (mann is to think). Refers to sacred chants. Gurumantra is the sacred and ceremonial imparting of important clues from the guru to the shishya.

Masaknaa: A feeling of movement after dullness in a performance. Also used when flexibility and lucidity are experienced as the voice, as well as the mind, are warmed up.

Maseetkhaanee: A particular type of gat on the sitar, attributed to Masit Khan, whose son is said to have been attached to the court of Wajid Ali Shah. The gat has its uthaan (starting point) essentially on the twelfth beat of the teentaal but it is heard in other taals also, in both vilambit and madhya layas.

Matt: School of thought and belief. In ancient times there were three schools of musical thought, known as Shivmatt, Hanumatt (Hanumanmatt) and Krishnamatt, named after the respective gods Shiva, Hanuman and Krishna. There is not much evidence today of what these schools stood for. However, certain ragas, for example, Shivmat Bhairav, Shivmat Bheempalasi and Hanumat Todee etc., at times indicate the different treatment of certain ragas. Even certain common ragas differed in interpretation according to these schools of thought (see also *Raga Deepak*).

Matt taal: See *Taal*.

Mazaameeree: A word used for an enjoyable (though not necessarily lighter) attitude while rendering, which is not heavily grammared.

Meend: A vocal expression in which an arch-like movement takes place between two notes. The reaching note is conceived of from the starting note. It may be via another note, which functions like another pillar in the arch. The same structure is called soot or ghaseet in instrumental music. Sometimes the expression soot is casually used to denote this shape, both vocally and instrumentally.

Meera: Famous saint-poet from Rajasthan (1559–1620), who was a great musician; born a princess, and a devotee of Lord Krishna, the raga Mirabai kee Malhaar is associated with her.

Mehfil: Chamber concert. Traditionally this was any intimate gathering for the purpose of listening to music. Also referred to as bazm.

Mel: Just as thaath in north Indian music is the basis of standardization of ragas, mel is a system of categorization that forms a base for standardization in Carnatic ragas. Mels are seventy-two in number, thirty-six from Madhyam teevra and thirty-six with shuddhmadhyam. Melkartaa are the ragas derived from mels.

Merukhand: Meru means 'spine'; khand means 'portion'. The Merukhand system discussed in the *Sangeet Ratnaakara* by Sharangadev is a mathematical ordering of notes through which 5040 taans are possible in seven notes (see also *Aman Ali Khan, Amir Khan*).

Milee bhagat: A mutual understanding, not necessarily in the positive sense, between two performers, generally instrumentalists (one of them the percussionist) before a performance with the idea of impressing the audience.

Miraasee: Comes from the word meeraas, which means 'inheritance'. Refers to the community of musicians who inherit their music.

Mishra raga: Mishra or mishrit means 'mixed'. Mishra raga is a specifically declared combination of generally two ragas.

There are generally two ways of mixing two ragas: either the first half (poorvaang) is one raga of the octave and the second half (uttaraang) is the other, or the complete aarohee is one raga and the complete avrohee is the other (see also *Sankeerna* and *Chaayaa lagat raga*).

Mithaas: Sweetness of the swara, generally used when a pinpoint-fine accuracy of the note is achieved.

Mitthaa besuraa: An expression in Punjabi. This refers to a typical state of tunefulness in a musician when he is never pinpoint correct and yet at the same time difficult to find fault with.

Mizaaj banaanaa: Mizaaj is 'temperament'. Phrase used generally for students during the period when they should sit among musicians and cultivate their minds, develop the musical temperament, as it were.

Mizraab: A cap made of copper or steel string worn on the first finger of the right hand to strike the sitar or veenaa. The different stroke-patterns made by this mizraab are also called mizraab.

Mohammad Shah 'Rangile': Mughal ruler of the eighteenth century, who was a great patron of music. Many compositions by Sadarang were dedicated to him.

Moorchhana: Moorchhana is essentially a linear formation of five, six or seven notes (no note being repeated). The order of notes suggests the raga. The changing of the base note shifts the order of the rest of the notes accordingly, to get at the skeletal form of another raga. The word comes from moorchh, meaning 'unconscious'. Moorchhana here would mean 'the subconscious'. When rendering a raga, apart from the conscious scale, the musician is also subconsciously aware of routes, indicating other raga scales within the raga he is performing. Moorchhana therefore means 'route'. Moorchhana paddhatee is the moorchhana system, and is used to refer to ragas derived from the moorchhana method.

Moordhaa: Upper portion of the jaw (the taaloo or palate) from where t and th are pronounced. This part of the mouth is supposed to be involved in the singing of taar saptak notes.

Morchang: A folk instrument consisting of a double metal flap, about 8–9 inches long, which is inserted into the mouth and played with the finger.

Mridang: Large percussion instrument (like the pakhaawaj) used in dhrupad singing as well as veenaa accompaniment. It has a majestic sound. Its left side is plastered with freshly prepared dough to give it a deep sound.

Mridangam: Another percussion instrument, a slightly smaller mridang, this is used in Carnatic music. Its left side, like the mridang, is also plastered with dough.

Mudraa: While singing or playing, the posture of a musician (used for dancers also).

Mudraa dosh: Mudraa dosh is a phrase often used for a postural defect in a musician while practising or performing.

Mughannee, Mughaneeyaa: A Persian word that has come from naghmaa, referring to 'a piece of music'. Mughannee is the male singer and mughanneeyaa refers to a female singer, both of whom narrate the naghmaa.

Muhaar: Comes from mukh or face. Refers to the size of the upper part of the tablaa, particularly the right one.

Mukhadaa: Literally, 'face'. Refers to the first part of any composition in khayaal, thumree, bhajan, geet or any other form which is used repeatedly (and is, so to speak, the 'face' of the song). Also called munh or muh.

Mukhya ang: The 'prominent part' of the raga, its grip or exclusive haunt, also called pakar (see *Pakar*).

Munh se bol kaatnaa: A proverb used among performers of duets, referring to the point when one vocalist completes the other's unfinished taan. It has a sense of wit about it.

Murkee-phandaa or murk: Short, crisp structure of two or three notes. Also known as gitkaaree.

Murlaa: Large flute. Unlike the muralee, which is a flute of ordinary size, it is blown and played straight, not sideways.

Mushtaq Hussain Khan: Musician of Rampur (Sehsawaan gharaanaa, 1872–1964). He had a resilient voice and was familiar with a wide range of compositions.

N

Naabhee swara: Naabhee is the umbilicus. Refers to vocal pressure on the diaphragm which produces a deep tone.

Naad: Naad means 'sound'. Also called Naada Bramha, for according to Indian mythology, it is a belief that when there was nothing, the first thing to be evoked was sound. That sound is Naad (see also *Om*).

Naagaswaram: Also naadaswaram, this is a very large, shehnaaee-shaped wind instrument of south India. An ancient instrument, according to one version it originated in the Nag community of ancient India, said to have existed even before the Aryans.

Naat: A devotional song in qawwaalee style.

Naatyashaastra: The ancient Sanskrit text written by the sage Bharata, about dance, drama and music, and said to be the fifth Veda told to Bharata by the Creator, Bramha himself.

Naayak: A martial word, which means 'leader'. At one time, any 'leading' musician of the times was referred to as naayak by the people in general, though not by the courts.

Naayikaa: The heroine in the theme of dance-dramas, as well as in many a lyric set to music.

Nagaadaa: Large martial drum played with two sticks. A set of nagaadaas smaller in size were traditionally used for accompanying the shehnaaee.

Naghmaa: Generally used to refer to any 'piece' of music. Naghmaasaar is the person who produces it (see also *Laharaa*).

Naktaa: See *Taal*

Namkeen: Literally, 'containing salt'. Used for a 'colourful' musical personality.

Naraawaaz: Nar is 'male'. Generally used for the power and grandeur of the male voice. The word narkanth is also used, which refers to the manly character of the voice.

Narad Muni: Celebrated sage in Indian mythology, who was a celestial singer. According to Hindu mythology, Narad Muni was a son of Bramha, who learnt the art of music from Lord Shiva, and taught it to Bharat Muni. The ancient historical musical texts mention many more Narad Munis and Bharat Munis.

The famous Sanskrit shloka, '*Naaham vasaamee vaikunthe, yoginaam hridayanucha, madbhaktaa yatra gaayantee, tatra tishthaamee Naaradaha*' is said to have been uttered by Lord Vishnu to Narad Muni in praise of music; the Lord himself said, 'I am not in Heaven, nor in the heart of yogis; I am where my bhaktaas (devotees) sing.'

Nat: Nat means 'actor'. The community of artists involved in dance and drama; also any member of the community bearing the same name.

Nataraaj: God of the nats, that is, Lord Shiva, also known as Nateshwar (see *Nat* above).

Nathnaa: Literally, 'nostril'. Refers to the correct nasal resonance in the voice.

Naudhaa: Nau is 'nine', dhaa here refers to sam. Any tihaaee repeated thrice in any taal (see *Teen tihaaee*).

Nausikhiyaa: Literally, 'newly learnt'. An inexperienced musician.

Nauras: Rasa means 'essence'. Nauras are the nine moods or rasas which mostly figure in dance and drama. These are: sringaara (gay), haasya (humourous), karunaa (pathetic or compassionate), raudra (angry), veera (valorous), bhayaanaka (fearful), bibhatsa (odious), adbhuta (wonderous) and shaanta (peaceful).

Nazrulgeetee: Songs written and composed by the Bengali poet Kazi Nazrul Islam, very popular in the Bengali-speaking belt.

Neechaa swara: Lower note (not to be confused with komol swara which refers to minor notes).

Neeras: Musically dry (see also Rookhaa).

Nigaahdaar: Nigaah is look. To have a good eye, in other words perception (in general) about music, also to be able to foretell the future of a promising musician.

Niggar: Richness and solidity in note as well as in the music.

Nikal-baith: Literally, 'the gimmicks' employed by heroic swordsmen. In music, this is used when going through difficult patterns with ease, meeting challenges successfully. Often used in connection with the thrill produced through a variety of taan patterns.

Nikaasee achchee hai: From the word nikaas, meaning 'to originate'. Used in praise of a musician who knows the secrets of (and has the ability for) producing with clarity and ease any bol on the tablaa.

Nikhaar: Literally, 'to bloom'. Refers to a 'blooming freshness' in music.

Nikhil Banerjee: Pandit Nikhil Banerjee (1931–1986) was a sitar maestro of the Maihar gharaanaa. A student of the legendary Baba Allauddin Khan, he was known for his technical virtuosity and clinical execution. His music was influenced by Ustad Amir Khan. Later, he also studied with Ustad Ali Akbar Khan. His usage of a completely bandh or 'closed' jawari in the Maihar style sitar allowed for much greater sustain, as can be heard in his unique sound.

Nipun: Perfect in the art (of music).

Nirgun: Same as niraakaar, meaning 'without form', or the Absolute; there are many devotional songs, mostly by Kabir and his followers (Kabeer Panthee) which are known as Nirguniaa or Nirguniaa bhajan.

Nishaad: The seventh note in the saptak. It is so called because the Nishaad, according to the Ramayana, were a community living on the Avadh border in ancient times. Nishaad therefore refers to border, and nishaad, in the saptak, is the border note (see also *Kaaklee nishaad*).

Nissar Hussain Khan: One of the latest of the old stalwarts, who belonged to the Rampur–Sehsawan gharaanaa, Nissar Hussain Khan (died1993), spent his last years contributing to the Sangeet Research Academy, Calcutta. He has left behind his heritage to his son Sarfaraz Husain Khan and his son-in-law Hafeez Ahmad Khan (see also *Sehsawan gharaanaa*).

Nok jhonk: A musically provocative exchange between two performers.

Nom tom: Aalaap at the beginning of dhrupad is called nom-tom aalaap (see *Dhrupad*).

Nyaas: The resting notes, or points of rest, allowed in ragas.

O

Okaar: Vocal practice that involves singing with the mouth shaped to produce the sound 'o' (see *Hoonkaar*).

Om: In music, a vocal accent covering swaras 'aa' and 'ao' (vowels in the Devanagiri script) and closing in with the vyanjan (or consonant) 'm'. According to Hindu belief this is the first sound of the Absolute, also called the sound of Naada Bramha. The production of this sound by the human voice covers the complete journey of sound itself, from 'aa' to 'm'.

Om Ananta Hari: The absolute or the infinite. This became a mantra chanted by dhrupad singers when they performed aalaap, evolving from the dummy words nom tom etc. (see *Mantra*).

Omkarnath Thakur: One of the foremost disciples of Pandit Vishnu Digambar Puluskar, Omkarnath Thakur (1897–1967) had a very melodious and powerful voice and an impressive personality. In emotional appeal, his style bore the influence of Ustad Rehmat Khan Bawle of Gwalior (who died in 1922). He wrote the texts *Sangeetaanjalee* and *Pranav Bhaaratee* and also many compositions under the pen name of Pranav Rang. He was the first dean of the music faculty at Benaras Hindu University.

His disciples include N. Rajam (the violinist), Balwant Rai Bhatt and P.N. Barwe.

Oparee taan: Oparee is from uparee, meaning 'superficial'. Refers to taan rendered without personal involvement.

P

Paaneekarnaa: To make lucid, like water. To practise any exercise to the point of maximum flow.

Padaavalee: Any collection of lyrics or padaas.

Paddhatee: A specific school of particular musical practice (see also *Pranaalee*).

Pahar: A duration of three hours. From the Sanskrit prahar, which has the same meaning. In a broad sense, it refers to time in general. In music, it is used for the time allotted to every Hindustani raga for the purpose of playing or singing, which is approximately three hours.

Pakar: This is the 'grip' of the raga. Refers to the most haunting and characteristic phrase or phrases of the raga, which convey its inner identity. This is also known as the soul of the raga. The pakar is never repeated in any other raga, even though another raga may have the same notes (to understand this further see *Ragavaachak*).

Pakhaawaj: A two-faced percussion instrument which accompanies the veenaa or dhrupad-dhammaar singing. The instrument is played with open hands; freshly prepared dough, made from flour, is plastered on the left side to deepen the tone.

Pallavee: Used in Carnatic music for the 'expansion' of the composition. Comes from the Sanskrit word pallav, meaning to 'come to new leaf', or in other words 'to adorn'.

Panchaalee: Folk form from Bengal.

Pancham: Fifth note of the octave.

Pandaal: Makeshift open-air auditorium prepared with tents to accommodate large audiences for music festivals.

Paran: A particular bol on the tablaa or pakhaawaj.

Pardaa: Fret in English (see *Saarikaa*).

Pannalal Ghosh: Well-known flautist, disciple of Ustad Allauddin Khan, Pannalal Ghosh (died 1960) intoduced a very large flute for playing, which provided a heavy base for ragas. One of his disciples is his son-in-law, Devendra Murdeshwar.

Parveen Sultana: Begum Parveen Sultana (1950) is a Hindustani classical vocalist of the Patiala gharaanaa. Her father, Ikramul Mazid, was her first guru. She later learned music from Birendra Kumar Phukan, Hiren Sarma, and Pandit Chinmoy Lahiri. She was also groomed in Kirana by her husband, Ustad Dilshad Khan.

Patiala gharaanaa: A famous gharaanaa of Punjab, though an offshoot of the Gwalior school. Originally a family of musicians from Kasur, a small tehsil of Lahore district (in Pakistan) they served at the court of Patiala, from where the school got its name. The well-known musicians of this gharaanaa were Fateh Ali (with the title of Taan Kaptaan), Ali Baksh (with the title of Jarnail, and in fact the two were also known together as Alia Fattoo), Kale Khan, Mian Jan, Bade Ghulam Ali Khan, Akhtar Hussain (son of Fateh Ali) and Ashiq Ali Khan (son of Ali Baksh Jarnail). The chief characteristics of this gharaanaa are its sparkling, toneful aakaar; small and intricate taan structures sustained within few notes; and thrilling, flash-like sapaat and choot taans.

Patraa: The piece of leather on the tablaa baayaan or pakhaawaj.

Peepnee: A very small flute, played in the folk music of the Punjab.

Pen names: Through pen names, composers of the khayaal bandish have often reflected their attitudes towards music. Harrang and Sab-rang, for instance, are pen names which convey the thought that the composers sang and composed 'in all colours', (rang meaning 'colour'); Sur-rang, the pen name of Ustad Amir Khan, conveys that Khan Saheb's innermost quest was the 'colour of swara'; Mitu-rang, which I chose for myself, is ultimately a Sufi expression—seeing the Lord in the shape of a friend. Pranay-rang, the pen name of Pandit Omkarnath Thakur, means 'the colour of Om', Pranav being another name for 'Om'. Similarly, Prem Piyaa (Ustad Faiyaz Khan), Akhtar Piyaa (Nawab Wajid Ali Shah), Praana Piyaa (Vilayat Hussain Khan), Daras Piyaa (Mehboob Khan), Vinod Piyaa (Tasadduk Hussain Khan) and Madhur Piyaa (Goswami Gokulutsavji Maharaj)—'piyaa' in all these cases conveys a feeling of belonging and identification (with its undertone of heroism) with the 'beloved', who is conceived of as the abstract 'prem', 'praana', 'vinod' and so on.

Peshkaar: Improvisation of the introductory bols of the tablaa. The rest of the bol—gat, paran, relaa etc.—are played subsequently.

Phaag: The songs related to the Festival of Holi, which comes in the month of phaagun or March.

Phailaao: The expansion of the raga (see *Badhat*).

Phandaa: A word used along with murkee (usually as murkee-phandaa), for small, knot-like phrases in music (see *Murkee*).

Phirat: Comes from the word phirnaa, 'to wander about'. Refers to the free movement of the taan through the scale (see *Tanaitee*).

Pitch: To fix the key (according to the musician's personal convenience). This English term has been absorbed into Hindustani music terminology as no other equivalent of the term is available (see also *Introduction*).

Poorab baaj: The tablaa styles of Farakkabad-Ajrada, Lucknow and Benaras (all in Uttar Pradesh) are known as Poorab baaj. The special characteristics of these styles are as follows:

- ***Benaras:*** The tablaa players trained in this style play with their hands comparatively wider open. The baayaan is slightly tilted towards the daayaan, the result is that the bol of dhaa sounds ghaa; in the same way ghig-ghig, etc., are also produced.
- ***Farakkabad-Ajrada:*** Named after the twin townships bearing the same name, the speciality of these styles is the special laya-variations on the tablaa. The Ajrada style is very conducive for dance forms.

- **Lucknow:** This has a distinct influence of Delhi baaj, with a special emphasis on the thaap bol.

Poorvaang: The first half of the raga; its range is from Saa to Maa or to Paa (see also *Hindustaani raga, Uttaraang and Vaadee*).

Potaa: Potaa are the ends of the fingers, from tips to the first knuckles, used in the playing of the saarangee, israaj, sarod, and so on (see also *Potaa badaa sur mein hai,* under *Daad*).

Prabandha: The Sanskrit *'prakrishta roopena bandhaaha'* means, 'that which is perfectly composed is prabandha' (prakrishta means well-knit or perfect, roopena is 'the way', and bandhaaha (or bondage) here means composed. Prabandha means 'arrangement'. Refers to the overall arrangement of swara, raga and taal. Any form in Hindustani music will be based on these three main aspects. Any gaayakee based on these aspects will be prabandha gaayakee. Prabandha gaan also referred in ancient times to songs composed for naatak or drama.

Prabha Atre: Dr Prabha Atre (born 1932) is a living legend of the Kirana gharaanaa. Besides being an accomplished performer, she has also excelled as a brilliant thinker, researcher, academician, reformer, author, composer and guru. She is specially hailed for the ways she uses sargam and gamak from Carnatic music to enrich her rendition. Her gurus were Sureshbabu Mane and Hirabai Badodekar. She drew inspiration from the styles of the maestros Amir Khan and Bade Ghulam Ali Khan.

Pranaalee: The active following of a musical tradition (see *Paddhatee*).

Praana Piyaa: Pen name of Ustad Vilayat Khan of the Agra gharaanaa (see also *Pen names*).

Pudee: The leather top of the tablaa or pakhaawaj (also called Patraa).

Pungee: A snake-charmer's flute.

Prachalit raga: Prachalit is 'that in practice'. A lesser-known raga is an aprachalit raga.

Pukaar kee taan: Pukaar means 'to call'. Used for the haunt ending with an echo, and leaving its tail-note on some other nearer or distant note.

Q

Qalab bolnaa: Literally, 'as if the soul itself were singing'.

Qalbaanaa: Qalab is the word for soul in Urdu. Qalbaanaa, the Sufi verse relating specifically to the soul, is sung in qawwaalee style (see *Qawwaalee*).

Qawwaal Bachche: The musicians who initially introduced the qawwaalee style of singing. Hazrat Amir Khusro was one of the foremost followers of the Qawwaal Bachche tradition (see *Qawwaalee, Chishtee Paramparaa*).

Qawwaalee: The word comes from qaul, which means 'the sayings of saints', here mostly Sufi saints. The qawwaalee form originated in the thirteenth century; a group of singers, followers of Khwaja Moinuddin Chishtee Garib Nawaz of Ajmer, known as Qawwaal Bachche, used the existing forms of Indian music to spread the message of Sufism. Thus came about a distinct qawwaalee style. The taan, aalaap, paltaa, bol, even sargam are elements of Indian music that can still be traced to the qawwaalee style (see also *Qalbaanaa*).

The earliest form of the Persian ghazal and the drut compositions of khayaal, known as chotaa khayaal, had the same musical elements as the qawwaalee but became distinctive as a result of the difference in their poetical forms (see *Chishtee paramparaa*).

R

Raagee: A community of shabad singers employed in gurudwaaraas (see *Shabad*).

Raas: A musical dance-drama about young Lord Krishna and his gopees which originated in Braj, where Lord Krishna was brought up.

Raavanahattaa: An earlier version of the saarangee, which had fewer strings. It is a folk instrument.

Raga: The word raga, translated roughly, means 'love'. *Ranjayatee itee ragaha* means 'raga is that which pleases' (aesthetically). The raga forms the basis of Indian classical music; it is a musical scheme of five, six or seven notes composed logically, the layout of the notes evolves into a significant form. Each note has its own accent, each raga its own rules that are to be followed strictly.

Every raga has also its own peculiar haunt or grip (pakar); the grip of one raga is never the same in another. Two or more ragas may have the same notes but not the same grip. This grip identifies the character of the raga (see *Pakar*).

Ragang paddhatee: This categorizes ragas in a way similar to the thaath school of standardization. The concept has been introduced by Vinayak Rao Patwardhan in his Raga Vigyaan series, and is mostly observed by the Gandharva Mahavidyalaya school.

Ragadyotak: Same as *Ragavaachak.*

Raga khulnaa: Khulnaa is to 'open out'. Refers to the clear picture of the raga.

Ragamaalaa: Maalaa is 'garland'. Ragamaalaa is a composition in which various ragas are presented, one after another. The main mukhraa is reverted to again and again (see *Ragasaagar*).

Raga rasoee paagaree, kabhee kabhee ban jaaye: Raga here is 'music', rasoee is 'cooking', paagaree is 'turban'; a saying which means that things of this nature can only at times, and not always, come to perfection.

Raga-reet: The customary or traditionally observed details of the raga, both in the grammatical as well as in the aesthetic sense.

Raga-roop: A final 'picture' of the raga.

Ragasaagar: This is almost the same as ragamaalaa, but composed.

Ragavaachak: A short, distinctive phrase common to a family of ragas. For example, Re, Gaa, Re, Saa, with Re and Gaa komal is the ragavaachak for all Todees; Gaa, Maa, Re, Saa with Ga komal will be ragavaachak for all Kaanhadaas; Maa, Re Paa will be ragavaachak for all the Malhaars, and its reverse, Paa Re Maa will be ragavaachak for all the Saarangs (with the exception of Gaur Saarang), and so on.

Rabaab: A wooden sarod-like instrument. The sarod is a further improvisation of the rabaab.

Rabaabee: This was a community of musicians in Punjab before the partition of India and Pakistan. They were descendents of Baba Mardana, a disciple of Guru Nanak. Rabaabees, as they came to be known, were attached to gurudwaaraas. They represented a very gentle mingling of Sikh, Muslim and Hindu cultures.

Rabindrasangeet: Songs written and composed by the famous Bengali poet, Rabindranath Tagore.

Rajab Ali Khan: Great khayaal singer, born in Narsinghgarh in 1874. Son of the saarangee player Mughal Khan, Ustad Rajab Ali Khan came to settle in Devas near Indore. A special feature of his music was the ability to render chootor sapaat taans in the most complicated (sankeerna) ragas with the ease of any simple scale. Among his disciples were Shankar Sarnaik and Ganesh Ramchandra Behre Buwa. He died in 1959.

Rajan-Sajan Mishra: Pandit Rajan Mishra (born 1951) and Pandit Sajan Mishra (born 1956) are renowned vocalists in the Khayaal style of the Banaras gharaanaa of Hindustani classical music. The brothers received their initial training from their grandfather's brother Bade Ram Das-ji, their father, Hanuman Prasad Mishra, and from their uncle, Sarangi maestro, Gopal Prasad Mishra. Their disciples include Ritesh Mishra, Rajnish Mishra, Diwakar, Prabhakar, Viraj Amar and Dr Shalini Sinha.

Rajwaadaa: Estate of a rajah during feudal times; musicians were maintained at these rajwaadaas or courts.

Ramkrishna Vaze Bua: Well-known musician of the Gwalior gharaanaa, Vaze Bua was most respected among the musicians of Maharashtra and given the title of Naveen Tansen.

Ram Narayan: Pandit Ram Narayan (born 1927) popularized sarangi as a solo concert instrument in Hindustani classical music. He is associated with the Kirana gharaanaa through Ustad Abdul Wahid Khan. Most of his compositions are from the singing repertoire of his teachers and were modified and adapted to the sarangi. Known for his mastery of Sur he has developed compound ragas and made the sarangi known as a solo instrument. His well-known disciples are sons Brij Narayan and Harsh Narayan, daughter Aruna Kale, and S.L. Khandara.

Rampur gharaanaa: An offshoot of the Gwalior gharaanaa; according to the musicologist Acharya Brihaspati, Wazir Khan Saheb, Allauddin Khan, Hafiz Ali, Ali Akbar, Ravi Shankar and Amjad Ali Khan are all musicians of the Rampur or Seniya gharaanaa. The Rampur gharaanaa was a major reference point for Bhatkhande, who received a great deal of material from the Rampur musicians for his collected works (see also *Tansen, Seniya gharaanaa*).

Rang: Means 'colour'. From 'rng' which means 'to attract with colour'. Here, a form of qawwaalee. Any of the stanzas can be frequently changed from one raga to another. This is more or less like ragamaalaa or ragasaagar, which are sung in the khayaal style (see *Ragasaagar, Ragamaalaa*).

Rangeelaa gharaanaa: The Agra gharaanaa, so called because its musicians are the descendents from the court of Mohammad Shah 'Rangile' (see *Agra gharaanaa*).

Ranjan: To please or to entertain.

Rasa: Literally, 'to take pleasure'. The word is used for the total experience of music heard and felt (see also *Nauras*).

Raseelaa: Very tuneful.

Rasik: A lover of music.

Rasiaa: A person fond of music. Also a folk form from Uttar Pradesh.

Raskhan: An Afghan Muslim and a Krishna bhakta, who lived in Brindavan and wrote hundreds of dohaas in Brajbhaashaa in praise of Lord Krishna, which are sung widely to this day.

Rasoolan Bai: A very fine thumree gaayikaa of Benaras gharaanaa (Poorab ang). She was the disciple of Shammu Khan.

Ratanjankar, S.N.: Musicologist and musician, the disciple of Pandit V.N. Bhatkhande and Ustad Faiyaz Khan, Professor Srikrishna Narayan Ratanjankar (1900–1974) was principal of Maurice College, Lucknow, then chief advisor for the first committee instituted for the gradation of classical musicians at All India Radio. A new raga, Saalakworalee, was thought out by him. He died on 13 February 1974, the same day on which Ustad Amir Khan passed into Naadaloka.

Ravish: Style.

Ravi Shankar: World-renowned sitar maestro and composer, Pandit Ravi Shankar (1920–2012) was a disciple of Baba

Allauddin Khan, the legendary founder of the Maihar gharaanaa of Hindustani classical music. He developed a style distinct from that of his contemporaries and incorporated influences from rhythmic practices of Carnatic music. He promoted the jugalbandi concert style and had a huge role to play in popularizing Indian classical music in the West. Prominent amongst his disciples are Jaya Biswas, Manju Mehta, Shubhendra Rao, Vishwa Mohan Bhatt and Anoushka Shankar.

Razaakhaanee: A type of sitar gat which is distinguishable by particular mizraab strokes.

Reengnaa: Literally, 'to crawl'. Used to suggest a dull, dragging effect in a performance.

Relaa: Relaa means 'surging crowds'. Here the word is used for the continuity of the crowd of bols on the tablaa.

Rishabh: Second note of the octave. The word comes from rish, which means 'to roar'; the word rishabh is used usually to refer to the bull. There is an association here. Before entering the temple of Lord Shiva, one passes Nandee the bull. Shadaj or Saa is supposed to be a representative of Lord Shiva. Similarly, to enter the domain of shadaj, which is a source for the seven notes, one has to pass through rishabh. The other association of this note and its name, rishabh, being compared with the snorting of a bull, seems vague.

Riyaaz: Comes from riyaazat, which means 'prayerful meditation'. Riyaaz refers to the musician's daily practice.

Rookhaa: Dry. A term denoting music that is not stirring in spite of being grammatically right.

Roohdaaree: Rooh is soul. Music which is inward.

Roopak taal: See *Taal*

Roshanara Begum: A famous musician from the Kirana gharaanaa (disciple of Ustad Abdul Karim Khan), she settled in Pakistan after the partition. She was, in the true sense of the word, taiyyaar (see *Taiyyaaree*).

Rubaaeedaar taraanaa: Rubaaee is a complete expression of poetic thought, in one or two couplets, and the taraanaas in which rubaaees are sung are known as rubaaeedaar taraanaas. These were popularized by Ustad Amir Khan (see also *Taraanaa, Amir Khan*).

Rudra veenaa: Also known as been; a large, hollow bamboo, without a knot, forms the body of this string instrument, and two large equal-sized toombaas are fixed on either side. The main string (baaj) is fixed on the reverse side, to get more space for the meend. The mizraab strokes are rendered accordingly. The frets are fixed with wax to avoid any kind of metal work (except for the strings themselves) on the bamboo. (Rudra is one of the names of Lord Shiva. This veenaa is one of the most melodious of the ancient Indian instruments.)

S

Saadhaaranee: From dhaaranaa, which means 'to conceive an idea'. According to the musicologist Thakur Jaidev Singh, saadhraanee is the earliest form of khayaal, even before dhrupad, which covers all the elements of musical expression found in khayaal today.

Saadhanaa: From the root saadh, which means 'to achieve'. 'Naa' here refers to 'effort'. Saadhanaa thus refers to 'the state of achieving or practising through effort', in other words through a continuing process of practise and realization. This is the connecting word in a three-word concept: saadhya, saadhanaa and siddhee. Saadhya is the 'aim', saadhnaa the 'practise' (upon the aim) and siddhee is 'the attainment' (siddh is 'the person who has attained'). Swara saadhanaa is the yogic concentration on and contemplation of the swara.

Saadraa: A khayaal composition in jhaptaal, the word saadraa is from sehdaaraa, which means 'three doors' or three points of entry into the domain of the taal. Jhaptaal has three taalees.

Saaf kar diyaa: To have washed away an earlier effect of music.

Saakhee: From saakshee, means 'witness'. Refers to sayings of the saints, which were sometimes also sung. These were used also as points of reference for people in general.

Saamgaan: Saam is from the root sam, which means 'balance'. Gaan is from gayee, which means 'that which can be sung'. Refers to the verses of the Saamveda, which are meant for singing. The verses of saamveda are the first verses mentioned in meters or laya. This is why they are supposed to be suitable for singing (there is the Sanskrit explanation for saam: *samasya bhaavaha saam*, which means 'all bhaava is saam', or 'balanced').

Saaranaa: Also known as tarab. These are the helping strings, tuned to a particular thaath. They lie below the main playing strings in the sitar, saarangee, israaj, surbahaar and sarod and among the veenaas the vichitra veenaa.

Saarandaa: A rabaab-shaped instrument played with a bow. Very loud and high-pitched, it is popular in Afghanistan.

Saarangee: The most popular bowing instrument for music accompaniment, now popular as a solo instrument also. It is the improved form of Raavanahattaa, a folk instrument from Rajasthan.

Saarikaa: Frets or ridges on the fingerboard of the sitar, surbahaar, Saraswati veenaa, rudra veenaa or dilrubaa. These are usually made of metal; however, in the rudra veenaa, they are of wood.

Sab-rang: The pen name of Ustad Bade Ghulam Ali Khan (see *Bade Ghulam Ali Khan,* and *Pen names*).

Sab-ras: Music with all kinds of styles.

Sadaa: Means 'haunt'. Mostly used in the context of vocal music. The proverb, *sadaayen aanaa*, is often used when indicating or recalling memories of (musical) haunts.

Sadarang: Pen name of the well-known khayaal composer Niamat Khan, who was a musician at the court of Muhammad Shah 'Rangile' (1719–1748). He was one of the musicians responsible for popularizing the khayaal and is credited with hundreds of khayaal compositions.

Safedee: Means 'white'. To play the highest notes on the saarangee, touching its skin covering, which is white.

Sain Karim: Famous musician of the Sham Chaurasi gharaanaa, grandfather of Salamat Ali (of Pakistan), Sain Karim served at the court of Jammu and Kashmir. One of the most sensitive and tuneful musicians of his day, Sain Karim was known to have become mentally unbalanced in the last few years of his life. Bhaskar Bua Bakhle said of him: 'If I was blessed with such a tuneful voice, I would have lost my senses too.'

Sakadee taan: The word sakadee comes from saankaree, meaning 'complicated'. Refers to the taan which involves a tremendous amount of skill in rendering.

Sam: The word, approximating 'equal', refers to a state of equilibrium, reached at sam. Sam is the first beat of the beat cycle of any taal. Naturally, the first beat is emphasized or shown distinctively when one circle is over.

Sampooma jaatee: Used when all seven notes are used in a raga (see *Jaatee*).

Samta Maharaj: Pandit Samta Maharaj, also known as Gudai Maharaj (1921–1994), was a renowned tablaa maestro from the Banaras gharaanaa. Trained by his father, Pt. Hari Sunder, grandfather, Pt. Jagannath Mishra, and Pt. Bikku Maharaj, he was the winner of many prestigious awards. His disciples of note are Shashanka Bakshi, Pt. Bhola Prasad Singh, Naba Kumar Panda, Gurmit Singh Virdee, Partha Sarathi Mukherjee, Rahul Dev Burman, Nitin Chatterjee and Pt. Kumar Lal Mishra.

Samvaadee: Vaad is to speak. Samvaad is to have a dialogue. Samvaadee refers to the note or notes to which vaadee speaks, or the forth or fifth note from vaadee. The status of samvaadee in the raga should, essentially, be the same as that of vaadee (see also *Vaadee*).

Sandhee prakaash raga: Sandhee means 'pact'. Sandhee prakaash refers to the moments when two times meet, that is, dawn and dusk. Hindustani ragas which are sung during those two periods are sandhee prakaash ragas.

Sangat: Accompaniment. The word conveys a sense of togetherness as well. This is also referred to as sangat-saath (saath means 'together').

Sangeet: The word break-up here is sam and geet. Sam means 'together' and geet means 'material for singing'. Earlier the word included music, song and dance. But now it is used only to refer to music.

Sangeet goshthee: A musical 'at home' with an intimate audience, a kind of soiree (see also *Mehfil*).

Sangeetopaasnaa: From upaasanaa, which means 'to meditate'. Refers to the attitude of devotion while practising music.

Sangeet shaastra: Shaastra can be broken into shaas, which means 'to rule', and tral, means 'to protect'. Refers to the authoritative text (usually scripture, though here a text on music), by which knowledge is protected through various prescribed rules and regulations.

Sankeerna raga: From sankar, means 'to mingle'. The sankeerna raga is a compound of more than two ragas. The difference between sankeerna and chaayaa lagat ragas is that the former is a clear mingling of various melodies and the latter contains diffused shades of other ragas (see also *Mishra raga* and *Chhaayaa lagat raga*).

Santoor: A harp-like instrument played with sticks in both hands. Originally a Kashmiri folk instrument, it is now used to play classical music as well. Known as kaanoon in Persian.

Sapaat taan: A straight, shooting taan (also called sattaa).

Sapardaaee: Comes from the Urdu sarpardaa, means 'that which is in the forefront'. Refers mostly to musicians who are important accompanists to the main performer. At times it is used for the teachers of singing girls, as well as their accompanists.

Saptak: The scale with a range of seven notes, Saa, Re, Gaa, Maa, Paa, Dhaa, Nee (see Ashtak, as well as the chapter titled

'Some Points of Controversy in Hindustani Music' for detailed explanation).

Saptasur: The saptak, or the seven notes, are also called saptasur.

Saraswati poojaa: Prayers offered to Goddess Saraswati, goddess of art and knowledge, also known as Bharati and Sharada. The root words in the word 'Saraswati' are sar (means 'lake') and rasa (means 'to take pleasure'. The poojaa takes place on the day of Basant Panchamee in early February. Mantras are chanted in praise of the goddess and rituals performed. White or yellow clothes are worn. White, being a symbol of purity, is associated with the goddess. Yellow symbolizes the season of Basant or spring, the period when Saraswati poojaa takes place.

Sargam: Although the word sargam comes from putting together the notes Saa, Re, Gaa, Maa, it refers to the rendering of music by the name of these notes (which is called sargam karnaa). For the Kirana, Bhendi Bazar and Indore musicians this is a special feature in their khayaal gaayakee. Sargam or singing while naming the notes helps to explain complicated patterns in music and works as a torch in the understanding of elaborate structures.

Sarod: A popular concert instrument in India today, the sarod is a variant of the Afghan rabaab. A steel plate is fitted on the fingerboard and with that the sound, unlike that of the rabaab, is metallic and loud (see *Rabaab*).

Savaal-jawaab: Literally, 'question–answer'. Used when equal phrases (with a minimum of three notes each) in uttaraang and poorvaang are in dialogue. This word is also used for a duet between two instruments, when their respective phrases build a heightened or dramatic question–answer 'climax'.

Sawaaree: See *Taal.*

Sawai Gandharva: Rambhau Sawai Gandharva (1886–1952) was a disciple of Ustad Abdul Karim Khan of the Kirana gharaanaa whose style bore a strong impression of his Ustad's gaayakee. Well-known disciples are Gangubai Hangal, Bhimsen Joshi and Feroze Dastoor.

Seedhaa thekaa: Seedha means 'straight'. To provide straight thekaa on the tablaa. This is a demand, usually of vocalists, to their tablaa accompanists for unimprovised beats on the tablaa to enable comfortable rendering.

Sehraa: Ceremonial song sung in praise of brides and bridegrooms during a wedding ceremony.

Sehsawan gharaanaa: One of the offshoots of the Rampur-Gwalior gharaanaa also known as Rampur-Sehsawan. One of its masters Ustad Nissar Hussain Khan died in 1993; his disciples are Sarfaraz Hussain Khan (son), Hafeez Ahmad Khan (son-in-law) and Rashid Khan (see also *Nissar Hussain Khan*).

Seniya: Name of the gharaanaa belonging to the traditions of Tansen. 'Sen' was added to the names of many musicians after Tansen, which is how the gharaanaa got its name (see *Rampur gharaanaa; Tansen*).

Shaadav: See *jaatee.*

Shaadav-odav: See *jaatee.*

Shaadav-sampooorna: See *jaatee.*

Shabad: Devotional songs from the *Guru Granth Sahib*, the Holy Book of the Sikhs. When in these songs the audience also joins in, it becomes shabad keertan.

Shadaj: First note of the octave. It forms the basis for the identification of the rest of the saptak. Comes from shataj, shata means 'six' and ja means 'born of' that is, 'born of six organs: nose, throat, chest, palate, the tip of the tongue and the teeth'. Shadaj, or Saa, is the point of origin of the other six notes. In Hindu mythology the note is supposed to be a representative of Lord Shiva.

Sham Chaurasi: A gharaanaa of musicians (sometimes called shaameeye) from the small town of Sham Chaurasi near Hoshiarpur, Punjab. One of the most well-known musicians of this gharaanaa was Sain Karim (see *Sain Karim*).

Shankh: A conch-shell, used for ritual blowing; in ancient times it was used during wars and on the occasion of special announcements made by the rulers to the people.

Shanti Hiranand: Shanti Hiranand was born in Lucknow. She studied at the Music College, Lucknow, and later shifted to Lahore. Her training in music came from Ustad Aijaz Husssain Khan of Rampur. From 1957 to 1974 she received training in thumri, daadra and ghazal from Begum Akhtar of whom she was the senior-most disciple.

Sharangdev: The scholar of music (1175–1247), who wrote the *Sangeet Ratnaakara*, the most authentic and uncontroversial among ancient texts on music. The special feature of the book is that is explains the system of Merukhand, under which 5040 taans can be concieved in seven notes without repetition.

Shehnaaee: The oboe-like blowing (wind) instrument, with a loud, piercing sound; the shehnaaee is associated with auspicious occasions.

Shishya: From the root shish, which means 'to hurt'. Shishya means 'disciple', him 'who is to be hurt to be disciplined', or him 'who exerts for discipline'. Shish also means 'to leave behind as a remainder', that is, to leave behind knowledge or a part of the guru in the shishya.

Shiv Kumar Sharma: Pandit Shiv Kumar Sharma (born 1938), renowned maestro and music composer, brought santoor, the folk instrument of Jammu and Kashmir, into the world of Hindustani classical music as an instrument of solo presentation. His training in tablaa and vocal music began with his father, Pandit Uma Dutt Sharma, at the tender age of five. His training in santoor began at age thirteen. He has contributed greatly to world music and fusion music. His disciples include Satish Vyas, Nandkishor Muley and R. Visweswaran.

Shloka: A Sanskrit stanza of poetry consisting of four lines.

Shori Mian: Master who was associated with tappaa gaayakee (the tappaa form of singing). Originally from Lucknow, Shori Mian whose actual name was Ghulam Nabi, settled in the Punjab and was a contemporary of Nawab Asifuddaulah. He has hundreds of tappaa compositions to his credit which celebrate his love for Sona, who is also said to have added to his compositions.

The legend goes that Shori Mian was told of Sona's wish to test his love: if he could lie down with a hot griddle (tavaa) on his chest, his love for her was true. And that is how Shori Mian died. Sona, when she heard of the tragedy, lost her sanity (see also *Tappaa gaayakee*).

Shobha Gurtu: Shobha Gurtu (1925–2004) was a highly acclaimed Hindustani classical vocalist who received her initial instruction from her mother Menakabai Shirodkar. Though she had equal command over the pure classical style, she became renowned for her rendition of the light classical music style. Besides thumri, she also excelled in dadras, ghazals and other forms.

Shringa: Means 'horn'. When a horn is used to blow, in music, the sound is called shringee naada.

Shrutee: From 'shru', meaning 'to hear' and 'tin' meaning 'to use'. The Sanskrit *shruyate itee shrutee* means—'shrutee is that which can be made audible (to others)'. In music there are twenty-two identifiable shrutees in the saptak. The seven notes are fixed on the fourth, seventh; ninth, thirteenth, seventeenth, nineteenth, and twenty-first shrutee s.

The difference between shrutee and swara (note) is that the latter is essentially a 'pleasing' shrutee. The basis for a pleasing shrutee is an even division between the shrutees (the distance or division being 4, 3, 2, 4, 4, 3, 2, madhyam being the 4 at the centre).

There are said to be innumerable shrutees, which cannot be pinpointed or identified by the human ear.

Shuddh: Pure. Any shuddh swara or note is the normal note, without any modulation of its natural placement.

Siddheshwari Devi: Well-known thumree exponent of the Benaras gharaanaa (1903–1977), Siddheshwari Devi was a disciple of Bade Ramdas.

Sikhyaa, dikhyaa, parkhyaa: It is said that music can be learnt in three ways—sikhyaa which means 'learning', dikhyaa implying 'observation', and parkhyaa which means 'practical application or practise' where what you learn or observe are put to test.

Singh Bandhu: The brothers Tejpal Singh and Surinder Singh are among the leading exponents of Hindustani classical music who received their early training in the Patiala and Kirana styles from their elder brother G.S. Sardar. Later they studied the finer nuances of Indore gaayakee under Ustad Amir Khan. The Singh Bandhu have made a significant contribution to Gurbani, the devotional music, by composing music for shabads.

Sitaar: One of the most popular of the Indian string instruments, its original name is sehtaar; seh means 'three' in Persian, and taar is 'string'. It was originally a three-stringed instrument (see also *Amir Khusro*).

Soolfaakh: See *Taal.*

Soot: See *Meend.*

Srot: Literally, 'fountain'. The source of continuous flow of music; used specially in the spiritual context.

Stotra: From the root stu referring to the 'essence of a deity'. A Sanskrit shloka or couplet, mostly narrated, is used to describe a deity. Stuti, on the other hand, is the shloka used in 'praise of the deity'.

Suhaag: Ceremonial song with good wishes for the bride.

Sujaan or surjan: A knowledgeable musician; the difference in the pronunciation of these two words is one of dialect.

Sundaree: A small shehnaaee-like instrument popular in Maharashtra.

Sur: Note (see *Swara*).

Surat: A spiritually preoccupied state of mind of the musician. According to Kabir, surat refers to anhada naada, the sound which is experienced without outer effort.

Surbahaar: A large sitar with thick strings and heavy frets, it is used for aalaap, jod and part of jhaalaa. All technique is the same as that for the sitar, and any sitar player can handle the surbahaar. It offers comparatively more scope for heavy, slower-paced work.

Surdas: The great poet and devotee of Lord Krishna (1535–1640), who wrote hundreds of songs which are part of the Krishna lore. His collected works are known as Sursaagar and Bhramar-geet. The raga Soordaasee Malhaar, is said to have been created by him. It is said that Surdas, whose name was Bilva Mangal, pledged to complete savaa laakh (125,000) songs in praise of Lord Krishna. When he was unable to do so, his disciples took over the task after him and wrote under the name of 'Soorshyaam'. The legend goes that Surdas blinded himself so that he would not set eyes on the material things of this world.

Sureelaa: Tuneful, as well as soulful.

Suresh Babu Mane: Suresh Babu (1902–1953) was a disciple of Ustad Abdul Karim Khan and Ustad Abdul Wahid Khan and younger brother of Heerabai Barodekar. He was very tuneful and melodious like Ustad Abdul Karim Khan.

Surmandal: Auto harp. A Western instrument, this has been incorporated into Hindustani classical music, mostly by vocalists; it helps to build atmosphere, constantly lighting up the scale.

Sur-rang: Pen name of Ustad Amir Khan (see *Amir Khan*).

Swara: The note. Swa means 'self' and raa is 'proferring'—swara therefore means 'a humble offer of the self'. Swara, in music, is thus an offering of the self through sound. In the Sanskrit and Devanagiri script, vowels are also known as swaras, based on the sanskaars or natural trends of the vocal mechanism. Vowels are known as swaras because sound originates in them (see also *Shrutee*).

Swara gyaana: Gyaana is 'knowledge'. Refers to well-practised sargam—or note-identification.

Swara-lipee: Notation of music.

Swayambhoo gandhaar: Swayambhoo can be split into swayam, meaning 'self', and bhoo meaning 'that which becomes' (by itself);

(also the third note in Western music; in fact the entire Western system revolves around the third and fifth notes).

The Sanskrit *swayam bhavate itee swayambhoo*, means, swayambhoo is 'that which becomes on its own'. Swayambhoo gandhaar refers to the hearing of the third note or gandhaar (audible by itself, as a natural resonance from kharaj or Saa).

T

Taa: A bol with the first finger on the edge (or kinaar) of the right piece (daayaan) of the tablaa.

Taal: From the root tal, meaning 'of the land'. The Sanskrit '*tal aghobhage*' means taal is 'sound on the ground'. In music, taal is the rhythm cycle containing the particular number of beats. It is also said that the word taal came from taa (for taandava) and laa (for laasya) (see *Taandava* and *Laasya*). Some of the commonly played taals are listed below.

- *Aadee taal:* A taal of eight beats used in the Carnatic system of music. The taalee falls on the first, fifth and seventh beats.
- *Aadhaa chautaal:* Two beats added to chaartaal or ektaal, making it aadhaa or odd. This taal therefore consists of fourteen beats. It is played on both tablaa and pakhaawaj (see *Chaartaal, Ektaal*).
- *Chaartaal or chautaal:* A taal circle of twelve beats played on the pakhaawaj, it has four taalees, on the first, fifth, ninth and eleventh beats, which is why it is known as chautaal. The third or seventh are khaalee (see also *Ektaal*).
- *Chanchal or Chaachar taal:* See *Deepchandee*.

- **Daadraa taal:** A taal of six beats, used in light or light classical singing. Its bol are Dhaa Dhin Naa, Dhaa Tin Naa.

- **Deepchandee:** A taal of fourteen beats, used mostly for thumree or light songs, it is also known as chanchal taal or chaachar taal. Its bol are Dhaa Dhin Dhin, Dhaa Dhaa Tin Tin, Taa Tin Tin, Dhaa Dhaa Dhin Dhin (see also *Jat taal*).

- **Dhammaar:** A taal of fourteen beats, played on the pakhaawaj and used in dhrupad singing. Its bol are Ke Dhee T Dhee T Dhaa Aaa, Ke Tit T Dhee T Taa Aaa.

- **Ektaal:** The taal of twelve beats played on the tablaa. This taal is the tablaa version of the chaartaal on the pakhaawaj. Its bol are Dhin Dhin, Dhaage Tirkit, Tin Naa, Katt Taa, Dhaage Tirkit, Dhin Naa-Naa.

- **Jat taal:** This taal is structured like deepchandee taal, but has sixteen beats. Thumrees are often sung in it. Its bol are Dhaa Dhaa Dhin-n, Dhaa Dhaa Tin-n, Taa-a Tin-n, Dhaa Dhaa Dhin-n. Ustad Abdul Karim Khan Saheb was very fond of singing in this taal.

- **Jhampaa:** This is a ten-beat taal and its khands are the opposite of Jhaptaal, that is, 3, 2, 3, 2. The bol are Dhin Dhin Naa, Tin Naa, Tin Tin Naa, Dhin Naa. This taal is used mostly in a lighter type of composition. Many Rabindra Sangeet compositions are found in this taal.

- **Jhampak:** This taal is half of jhampaa, that is, Dhin Dhin Naa, Tin Naa. Many Rabindra Sangeet compositions are in this taal. Also known as gaja jhampak (gaja means 'elephant'). It is similar to the elephant's gait.

- **Jhoomraa:** Comes from jhoomnaa, meaning sway. A taal of fourteen beats: its divisions are 3, 4, 3, 4. The taalee, naturally, is 1, 4 and 11. The khaalee is at 8. Its bol are

Dhin-n, Dha Tirkit, Dhin Dhin, Dha-ge Tirkit, Tin-n, Ta Tirkit, Dhin Dhin, Dha-ge Tirkit. However, in the modern jhoomraa there is no extra stay of first and eighth beats into second and ninth beats respectively. In other words, first and eighth beats are not prolonged into one and a half beats. This change was introduced by the Kirana and Indore musicians because the taal was used more for vilambit singing, and the extra stay could not sustain its subtle beauty.

- *Jhaptaal:* Taal of ten beats; the bol are Dhin Naa, Dhin Dhin Naa, Tin Na, Dhin Dhin Naa (see also *Saadraa*).
- *Keherwaa:* A taal of four beats, Dhaagee, Naatee, Nak, Dhin, used in folk or light classical music.
- *Khemtaa:* A folk variation of daadra taal (a taal of six beats).
- *Matt taal:* Matt means 'intoxication'. A taal of nine beats.
- *Naktaa:* Comes from nuktaa, which means 'secret point'. Refers to a taal of four beats.
- *Roopak taal:* A taal of seven beats used for almost all forms of music. The special feature of this taal is that its sam comes on khaalee. Its bol are Tin Tin Naa, Dhin Naa Dhin Naa. In Carnatic music, this taal is of six beats.
- *Sawaaree:* Literally means 'riding'. There are many sawaarees, taals mostly of odd-numbered beats: like the fifteen-maatra sawaaree, nineteen-maatra sawaaree, etc.
- *Sool taal* or *Soolfaakhtaa:* A taal of ten beats that gets its name from the faakhtaa bird, on the tempo of whose sound the taal is based. (Asool means 'principle'.) The taal has five khands, of two beats each. The bol are Dhaa, Dhaa, Dhin Taa, Kit Tak, Gatee Gin, and it is usually played on the pakhaawaj, being used in dhrupad gaayakee

or dhrupad-like straight compositions (see also *Amir Khusro*).

- ***Teentaal:*** The most popular taal of sixteen beats with taalee on first, fifth and thirteenth beats. Khaalee is on the ninth beat. Because of its three taalees, it is known as teentaal.

Taalee: Every khand (chamber) of any taal must have a taalee or khaalee on its first beat. This is to indicate the progress of the taal. Also called Bharee.

Taaleem: Literally, 'education', particularly practical training, from an ustad or guru.

Taan: The word comes from taananaa, meaning to spread, or to stretch. Refers to musical patterns rendered with speed; these can be short or extended (see *Tanaitee* and *Introduction*).

Taandav: Taand means 'to dance'. Taandava is the vigorous male dance, known as tandaav nritya, associated with Lord Shiva (see also *Laasya*).

Taankaa lagaanaa: Literally, 'to mend'. The covering up of expected lapses or mistakes in performance by an accompanist.

Taaoos: Literally, 'peacock'. Persian word, referring to the israaj, which has a peacock at its head.

Taar: String.

Taar saptak: Higher octave.

Taar shadaj: First note of the higher octave (see also *Teep*).

Taar shehnaaee: A small phonographic instrument fixed on top of the bridge of the israaj, producing a shehnaaee-like effect. This is why it is known as taar shehnaaee.

Taaseer: From asar, meaning effect. In other words music that has a deep (inner) impact.

Taashaa: A flat, earthenware drum, about half the depth of the baayaan of the tablaa, which is tied to the chest and played with two sticks. This is generally played during Muharram processions.

Tablaa: The most popular percussion instrument, consisting of a pair of drums, played in every type of north Indian classical music (except dhrupad, which uses the pakhaawaj). The right piece is tuned at the middle Saa and the left is supposed to be tuned at the lower Saa (this is usually not taken cognizance of). The tablaa pair is actually two separate halves of the pakhaawaj. Raw, hard leather, or kachhaa chamraa as it is called, is used in the making of tablaas.

Tablaa tarang: Ten to fifteen tablaas of the right hand alone (daayaan) are spread in a semi-circle, tuned on different notes and played with both hands open.

Tabeeyat lagnaa: To get in the mood to sing or play.

Tahreer: In Urdu, this refers to any handwritten material. In music, it is used to refer to oral notation (pronouncing the notes of musical structure), in other words, sargam.

Takraar: Any overlapping repetition of a sentence or a part of a sentence by a co-qawwaal in the qawwaalee.

Talwandi: Gharaanaa named after Talwandi, the town near Hoshiarpur. Maula Baksh and his son-in-law, Mehr Ali, and another disciple, Khaira, a famous clarinet player, were the musicians of this gharaanaa, which is no more.

Tambooraa: Also known as taanpuraa, this is the well-known instrument with four strings, used to provide the basic pitch. The two middle strings (jodaa) are tuned at middle Saa, the first string at lower Paa and the last, the thickest (made of brass or coiled), is tuned at lowest Saa, or mandra shadaj. The first string can also be tuned at Maa (madhyam) or Nee (nishaad). The tambooraas are played together to create the effect of continuous pitch. This is the single most important point of concentration for the musician. Sometimes, the same requirement for drone can be met when a group of musicians or disciples keep a basic, continuous humming pitch.

The word tambooraa is associated with the name of Tamburu Rishi, a sage of Vedic times. Tamburu Rishi was a disciple of Maharishi Narad. He is associated with the creation of the tambooraa, which was earlier known as the tamburu veenaa (see *Tambooraa*). The word taanpuraa can be broken into taan and pur, meaning 'to spread' or 'to continue' and 'to fill', respectively (see also *Aans*). Tun, a very light wood, is used in the making of both taanpuraa and sitar. The toombaa at the lower part is made with pumpkin, dried in the shade for several years together.

Tambooree: A tiny taanpuraa, which accompanies the sitar or sarod. Being a small instrument with tinier strings, it is tuned at a high pitch.

Tamburu: See *Tambooraa.*

Tanaitee: The entire aspect of taan portion rendered in khayaal; the same as phirat.

Tankaar: A stroke on any instrument.

Tanras Khan: Celebrated musician at the court of the last of the Mughal kings. There is a famous street in Old Delhi, still known as Taanras Khan kee galee. He created the famous Miyaan kee Todee composition, '*Kab moree naiyaa paar karoge*', in praise of Hazrat Nizamuddin Auliya. A gharaanaa, called the Tanras Khan gharaanaa, had followers like Mamman Khan, Chand Khan, Bundu Khan (saarangee nawaaz) and his son Umrao Khan (both settled in Pakistan), and Ramzan Khan (also in Pakistan). Unfortunately, the gharaanaa is now extinct. It was also known as the Delhi gharaanaa. Earlier this gharaanaa had some links with the Patiala gharaanaa.

Tansen: The most celebrated of court musicians, 'Miyaan' Tansen (1532–1595) was one of the 'nine jewels' at the court of Mughal Emperor Akbar. According to one version, he was originally Tanna Mishra, the son of Makrand Pandey, and the disciple of Swami Haridas. The ragas Miyaan kee Malhaar, Miyaan kee Todee and Miyaan kee Saarang are said to have been first thought out by him. He is said to have sung in Gauharee baanee. The Seniya gharaanaa musicians are said to be his descendants (see also *Bilas Khan*).

Tant: Comes from the word taant, meaning 'vein'. The word tant is used now for string instruments in general—the sitar, veenaa, etc. Animal veins are used in several instruments, like the saarangee, raavanahattaa and sometimes in the rudra veenaa also. A string instrumentalist is known as tantkaariaa.

Tappaa gaayakee: Comes from the Punjabi word taap, meaning 'to jump'. This is a beautiful form of classical singing in which bol and taan are thickly knitted at every possible step. With compositions in the Punjabi language, the tappaa is a creation of Shori Mian, and his beloved, Sona, whose names occur in most of the old compositions. Tappaas are very popular among musicians of the Gwalior gharaanaa (see *Shori Mian*).

Tappe: Verses based on the folklore of the Punjab. The first line, a dummy line having no meaning, keeps the metre. The second expresses the full meaning of the couplet, whether romantic or philosophic in flavour. These verses are sung in a straight, singsong tune.

Taraanaa: A very popular form in Hindustani classical music, it is slowly dying away. It contains Persian and Arabic phonemes like nom, dir, dir, taa, naa, naa, yallallah, yallallom, dernaa, deem, tadeem, etc.

There are several versions of the taraanaa. Some say that the phonemes were dummy words employed to convey Hindustani sargam or songs to Persian musicians, for whom the pronunciation and cultivation of flow in the sargam was very difficult. It also became popular at one time when it encouraged the spirit of competition between the dhrupad singer and veenaa player. Some of these words are very close, phonetically, to the veenaa and sitar accents.

Ustad Amir Khan was responsible for the revival of the taraanaa. He held that the taraanaa was nothing but a Persian song. He composed some Persian couplets in Hindustani ragas and wove them into his khayaal singing, particularly the fast khayaal. He pointed out that the phonemes were not meaningless, for example 'dar aa; dar aa' meant 'come unto me, come unto me', 'yallallom' meant 'Yaa Ali, Yaa Ali' and so on. As a result, however, of the alienness of the Persian language in the mainstream of the Hindustani tradition the taraanaa is becoming an archaic form (see also *Rubaaeedar taraanaa*).

Tarab: Helping (resounding) strings fixed below the main strings in the sitar, surbahaar, vichitra veenaa, israaj, saarangee, sarod, etc. They are generally tuned in the thaath of the raga which is to be played. When the strings are played, the helping strings resound tunefully.

Tarannum: Tarannum means 'narration'. Here, a monotonous tune in which Urdu poems are recited.

Taumbaa or toombaa: Large, dried pumpkin used in the making of sitar, taanpuraa, veenaa, etc.

Taiyyaaree: Same as taiyyaar, or mature. Refers to the maturity in a musician, when they are ready to be presented. Unfortunately, taiyyaaree now is equated with the speed of the taan of a musician.

Tar aawaaz: A lucid and tuneful voice.

Teen dhaa: Emphasizing every last beat of the three bols of the tihaaee, the third on the sam.

Teen tihaaee: Any tihaaee repeated three times, falling on the sam. Also known as Naudhaa.

Teep: Shadaj (Saa) of the higher octave. Also known as Teep kaa saa.

Teesree saptak: Third octave.

Teevra: Literally, 'high'. The word should be used only in reference to the higher Maa, but in practice teevra is used for any note that sounds higher than usual and is not right.

Teevra-tam: The sharpest note, both in tone and in the melody.

Teevra-tar: Sharp in tone as well as in the melody.

Tek or tek bharnaa: Refers to the refrain of a song, or the singing of that refrain.

Tetaree: An uncontrolled voice.

Thaap: This is an open-hand stroke on any percussion instrument: tablaa, dholak, mridang and pakhaawaj.

Thaath: A system by which ten different sets of eight notes each (sampoorna and one-sided or aarohee-wise) are formulated so as to categorize the maximum number of Hindustani ragas under it. According to Bhatkhande, there are ten thaaths. These are Bhairav, Todee, Kalyaan, Poorabee, Maarwah, Kaafee, Bhairavee, Aasaavaree, Khammaaj, Bilaaval. Most of the Hindustani ragas can be categorized under the ten-thaath theory. However, this categorization has its limitations. The thaath, as mentioned already, is essentially sampoorna, and one-way (aarohee). It could be said that thaath is to ragas what race is to the people of this world.

Thas: Literally, 'to fall flat'. Used mostly to refer to the voice.

Theka: Time circle (played on any percussion instrument).

Thiraknaa: Literally, 'to dance', especially with skilled foot movements. In music, this refers to any dance-like movement, accompanying great virtuosity on the tablaa.

Thirakwa: See *Ahmad Jan Thirakwa.*

Thumree: One of the lightest classical forms in Hindustani music, the word consists of thumak, referring to a gay, flippant gesture, and ree, meaning 'waalee', or 'belonging to'. In thumree the bol, mainly, is improvised in the same manner. There is not much taan, paltaa, sargam, aalaap or heavy classical innovation in this style. In thumree mostly shringaara, bhaktee and karunaa ragas dominate. In this style, ragas of lighter temperament are selected to match its own temperament, like Bhairavee, Khammaj, Peeloo, Kaafee, Tilang, Gaara, Jogiaa, Jhinjhotee.

Thumree is basically an attitude of presentation. It is apparently said to have Purab and Punjab ang. But in fact Purab ang is the authentic thumree, because not a single thumree or daadraa is available—or was ever composed—in the Punjabi language. Punjab ang is a folk flavour that is sometimes mixed into the Purab style.

Tihaaee: Three equal formations of a structure, the final point of which falls on the sam.

Tin: A bol of the right hand on the tablaa, played in the middle with the first finger.

Tirkit: A four-syllable bol (*t, r, ki, t*) produced on both pieces of the tablaa (see also *Dhirkit*).

Tirobhaav: When the raga is established during any performance, a musician can deliberately move into another raga for some time and return to the original one. This is known as tirobhaav (see also *Avirabhaav*).

Tirvat: Literally, 'three varieties'. A musical composition that contains sargam, tablaa bols and taraanaa.

Tissar jaatee: This is the quality of alankaar based on three- or six-note patterns.

Todaa: A small piece; usually played on the tablaa.

Tone: Although this is a word borrowed from the English language it has become a part of the language of Hindustani music today. Tonal consciousness has developed more after the introduction of the microphone. Refers to the weight of each note that has been cultured; this should be uniform throughout the music (see also *Introduction*).

Tootee: A small, flute-like blowing instrument with a very small range.

Tripallee: A three-piece bol on the tablaa.

Tulsidas: Celebrated saint–poet (died 1623), contemporary of Kabirdas, and a staunch devotee of Lord Rama, Tulsidas is the author of *Ramcharitmanas*, the most popular of the sacred books of the Hindus. It is arranged in the form of dohaas, chaupaaees and kaands, that is, couplets, four-line verses and categorized events respectively. This epic has traditionally been sung all over the country in one fixed dhun or tune.

U

Ucchaaran: Pronunciation of words as well as the accent of the swara.

Udaan: Literally, 'flight'. Musically, 'the flow of imagination'.

Ukaar: Practice of vocal singing 'o'-wise (see also *Aakaar, Eekaar, Hoonkaaretc*).

Ukhaad-pachaad: The competitive spirit between an artist and his accompanists (see also *Jugalbandee*).

Umadnaa: A surging flow of music.

Upaasnaa: The root word here is aas, which means 'to sit in worship'. It refers to the meditational stage of musical practice.

Upaj: Literally, 'to sprout'. Refers to a spontaneous creative expression.

Upnyaas: Short pause allowed on a particular note on the raga.

Upraga: Raga-s derived from a parental raga. In general usage, upraga has also become a concept of derivation in the sense that any raga conceived from another raga is upraga. However, ultimately all ragas when sung or played are independent entities (see also *Aadee raga, Janak raga*).

Upraant: To sing without interest and involvement.

Uthaa-pathak: Same as Ukhaad-pachaad.

Uthaan: Literally, 'to raise'. Used for the specific introductory piece of the raga (also called uthaav).

Uttaraang: The second half of the raga, it covers notes from Maa to Saa or Paa to Saa (see also *Hindustaani raga, Poorvaang* and *Vaadee*).

V

Vaadaa to pooraa karo: Vaadaa means 'promise'. It is said to a performer who introduces some complicated patterns and, without pursuing the challenge it poses, leaves it in between to start on to another pattern.

Vaadee: Comes from vaad, meaning 'to speak'. Refers symbolically to the note which 'speaks' for the raga. It has a dimensional value in the scale. For example:

- ***Bhairav:*** Saa, Re, Gaa, Maa, Paa, Dhaa, Nee, Saa; Re is samvaadee, Dhaa is vaadee.
- ***Eman:*** Nee, Re, Gaa, Maa, Paa, Dhaa, Nee; Gaa is vaadee, Nee is samvaadee.

In other words, any two equal bunches of three or four notes in the uttaraang and poorvaang and their pointed or 'speaking' notes (in respective or parallel situations) are considered as vaadee and samvaadee respectively (see also *Samvaadee*).

Vaaggeyakaar: Can be split into vaak, meaning 'to speak', gayee meaning 'to sing' and kaar referring to 'craftsmen'. In other words, the creator of a musical composition, who writes, composes and sings.

Vaanee: From vaach, meaning 'to speak'. Vaanee generally means 'speech' but is often used to refer to the sayings of the masters. For example, gurbaanee refers to the songs written by gurus or saints.

Vaishnav sangeet: Songs of saint–poets of the Vaishnav paramparaa, like Tulsidas, Meera, Narsi and others (see also *Havelee sangeet*).

Vakra jaatee: Vakra means 'twisted'. It refers to a category of ragas in which notes do not appear in linear formation.

Vakra swara: The note used but one that does not fall in linear formation in the scale of the raga (see also *Vikrit*).

Vakra taan: Any labyrinthine taan.

Vasantrao Deshpande: Dr Vasantrao Deshpande (1920–1983) was a Hindustani classical vocalist renowned for his contribution to Natya Sangeet. He learnt from several gurus, refusing to tie himself down to a single school of singing. He studied with Shankarrao Sapre of Gwalior, Sureshbabu Mane of Kirana gharaanaa, Aman Ali Khan Anjanibai Malpekar of Bhendi Bazar gharaanaa, Ramkrishna Vaze of Gwalior and Asad Ali Khan of the Khandar school of Dhrupad. Greatly influenced by Dinanath Mangeshkar, Dr Deshpande is regarded as the latter's sole musical heir.

Veenaa: Any instrument in the ancient times was called veenaa. The actual veenaa refers to the basic tuned instrument (the taanpura). The chalveenaa refers to an instrument that is re-tunable, on the achal veenaa or taanpuraa.

Vidwaan: Any learned musician. In south India particularly, musicians are known as vidwaans.

Vikrit: Complicated; used mostly in the stylistic sense. Vikrit swara is the note used in the raga but not directly, that is, pancham in the ragas Baageshwaree and Jog Kauns (see also *Vakra swara*).

Vilambit: From vilamb, which means, 'that which is kept in suspension'. Vilambit is slow. Used for badaa khayaal or slow gat on sitar and sarod.

Vilayat Hussain Khan: Well-known musician from the Agra gharaanaa (1862–1962). Apart from khayaal compositions he wrote ghazals as well and was considered a good composer with a vast knowledge of ragas. His pen name was Praana Piyaa. He was the author of *Sangeetagyon Ke Sansmaran*, in which he discusses the musicians of his time.

Vilayat Khan: Ustad Vilayat Khan (1928–2004), great sitar maestro of the Etawah-Imdadkhani gharaanaa, was also a composer, credited with the creation and development of gaayakee-ang on the sitar. He liked to perform without a taanpura drone, filling out the silence with strokes to his chikari strings. Inclined towards reinterpreting raagas and inventing new ones, he was first and foremost a traditional interpreter of spacious raagas such as Yaman, Shree, Todi, Darbari and Bhairavi. Several outstanding films have music scores created by him. His disciples include Pandit Arvind Parekh, Shahid Parvez, Shujaat Khan, Nishat Khan, Irshad Khan, Hidayat Khan, Budhaditya Mukherjee.

Vinay Chandra Maudgalya: Pandit Vinay Chandra Maudgalya (1918–1995) was a vocalist of the Gwalior gharaanaa of

Hindustani classical music trained by the stalwart Vinayakrao Patwardhan. In 1939, he founded Gandharva Mahavidyalaya, a music and dance academy in Delhi, to promote Hindustani music and Indian classical dances. One of his significant contributions to music has been the choir and the playful approach and simple syllabus he created to introduce children to the joys of raga music. Prominent students trained by him include Prakash Wadera, Satish Bhatia, Rekha Bhardwaj, Kailash Sharma and Prakash Saxena.

Vishnu Digambar Puluskar: Famous musician from the Gwalior gharaanaa (1872–1931), disciple of Balkrishna Buwa Ichalkaranjikar. V.D. Puluskar popularized music in society at large, especially in Hindu families, at a time when the musical profession lacked social respectability. He had many well-known disciples—Omkarnath Thakur, V.N. Patwardhan, Narayan Rao Vyas, B.R. Deodhar (whose disciple is Kumar Gandharva), and many others. His son, Dattatreya Puluskar, was also a fine musician, but died at a very young age.

Vishnu Narayan Bhatkhande: See *Bhatkhande.*

Vishraantee: Literally, it means 'to rest'. It refers to the pause or the interval between two musical phrases, which conveys a meaning. In other words, these phrases should definitely be knit together meaningfully through the pause.

Vistaar: From the root 'str', meaning 'to spread'. Aar here means 'entirely'. It refers to the expansion of the raga (see also *Badhat, Aalaap*).

Vitat: Any instrument without strings.

Vivaadee swara: Vivaad means 'to argue', or 'to clash'. Refers to the note which is not to be used in the raga—deliberately or by mistake.

Voice culture: This term, borrowed from the West, is now in common use among music circles of north India. It refers to the physical culturing of the voice (see *Saadhanaa*).

Vrindagaan: A choral song.

W

Wajid Ali Shah: Last Nawab of Oudh (1823–1887), a celebrated patron of the thumree and a great Krishna devotee, Wajid Ali Shah wrote many compositions and set them to music under the pen name of Akhtar Piyaa. Well-known thumree masters like Kalka Bindadin were at his court.

Z

Zamaane saaz gaanaa: To sing in the contemporary style or in the style that is in fashion.

Zameen banaanaa: Zameen is 'Earth'. Refers to preparing the base of the performance—the initial moments.

Zamzamaan: To shake the note, borrowing backwards as well as forwards (also a large martial drum played with two hard sticks).

Zarin (Daruwala) Sharma: Zarin Daruwala (born 1946), renowned sarod maestro, was a musical prodigy from age four. Her gurus were Pt. Haripada Ghosh, Pandit Bhishmadev Vedi, Pandit Laxmanprasad Jaipurwale, Pandit V.C. Jog, Dr S.C.R. Bhat and Dr S.N. Ratanjankar. Musician of the Agra gharaanaa, she was renowned for her rendering of aprachalit ragas with aprachalit talas with difficult layakari coupled with tayyari.

Appendix

Some Points of Controversy in Hindustani Music

I have long felt the need to throw light on certain controversies that have existed over issues critical to the understanding of our music, and that I have been discussing with my students and fellow musicians over the years. I would, therefore, not like to close the present dictionary without sharing with my readers as well these perceptions, especially since, in certain cases, the explanations to the same terms in the present text do not deal with the controversies surrounding them.

Saptak and Ashtak Concepts

On several occasions, I have come across confusion surrounding the saptak and ashtak concepts in our music. Apart from referring to the seven- and eight-note scales respectively, the terms saptak and ashtak are really concepts of measuring the scale, the measuring tapes used in both cases being different. It is like measuring with feet and yards on one hand, and centimetres and metres on the other. Saptak was an earlier method of measurement and since the introduction of Venkatamukhi's Melkarta as a base of standardization of the raga system, the ashtak (octave) came into existence.

The best way to understand the measuring would be to study the position of the middle note or madhyam. Madhayam means 'centre', and here it refers to the central note of the saptak or seven-note scale, with three notes on either side. Now in the octave, an eighth note is counted into the scale, though it has always existed before and not entered from outside. This is the first note of the next taar saptak, that is, Saa, which is just a double of the frequency of lower shadaj. Dividing these eight notes into two parts, Saa, Re Gaa, Maa, and Paa, Dhaa, Nee, Saa, let us see the position of madhyam or Maa. It was the exact central note of the saptak tape, though now it is the last note of the first half of the ashtak tape; fortunately it still bears the same name. Thus the ashtak in which the second half becomes just a repetition of the first half has brought about a change of concept and outlook in the Hindustani scale.

One would conclude that each of these concepts has its own culture of music, represented by its respective terminology. For example, graha and ansh are saptak terms whereas vaadee, samvaadee and anuvaadee are ashtak terms, though their functions may be more or less the same, technically speaking. But still, the clarity of concepts in the mind helps one to understand their formulae. While the study of terms such as graha and ansh provide us with clues to the treatment of ragas in the past, it is the vaadee-samvaadee of ragas that has been more important to the development of the raga in Hindustani music. However, sometimes terms of one concept are used to make explanations easier in the other concept.

Deshee and Margee Raga-s

Indian music is divided into two musical categories: maargee and deshee. Maargee is from mrg, meaning 'to search' (for a path).

And all paths are scientifically conceived. So maargee ragas are ragas that have been worked out, and fall under the classical category. Deshee, as its name suggests, is a category in which regional varieties, that is, folk music and folk-originated ragas, are to be found.

Despite the existence of these categories, too many misunderstandings prevail regarding our attitude towards folk-originated ragas. Let us take a few examples. Pahaaree is a deshee raga but Bhopaalee, with the same notes, is a maargee raga; Maand from Rajasthan is a deshee raga, but Nat and Bilaval are in the maargee category. Sindhee Bhairav is a deshee raga but Shuddh Piloo, and Kirwaanee with the same notes, are under maargee sangeet. As folk formations have no deliberate, rigid and specific scheme, deshee ragas are of the same flexibility, unlike maargee ragas, even though folk ultimately is the source of all maargee sangeet, in fact of all music. I mean Bhopaalee has been thought out from Pahaaree, Nat and Bilaaval from Maand, and Shuddh Piloo and Kirwaanee from Sindhee Bhairavee (all coastal notes, which to my mind are the most ancient haunts, right from Kerala to the Arabian coast. They include Shuddh Piloo of Maharashtra-Gujarat, Kirwaanee of the south and Sindhee Bhairavee of Sind.)

These were folk-originated ragas. As folk art involves no deliberate effort, the first definition of folk music is that it has no composer, its forms being directly related to its soil. So, when folk-originated ragas are sung or played, the freedom of the haunts should be maintained, keeping the raw shapes as they are. The confusion arises when we classify the folk through the classical, whereas in fact it should be vice-versa. Thus, Maand, Pahaaree, Sindhee Bhairavee and so on are folk dhuns which should not be considered as classical ragas of the maargee category.

Raga Deepak

From time to time the Indian raga system has been standardized in different ways. At one time a theory of six main ragas and thirty-six raginis, metaphorically referred to as their wives (six to each raga), became very popular. There were two schools which propagated this theory: the Krishna Matt and the Hanuman Matt. According to the theory, five of the six ragas are Maalkauns, Hindol, Megh, Shree and Bhairav. However, there was—and still remains—a controversy about the sixth raga in these schools; according to the Krishna Matt, the sixth raga was Nat; according the Hanuman Matt, it was Deepak. Now let us study the arrangement of these six ragas:

Krishna Matt		*Hanuman Matt*	
Megh	Saa, Re, Maa, Paa, Nee (Komal), Saa	**Megh**	Saa, Re, Maa, Paa Nee (Komal), Saa
Shree	Saa, Re (Komal), Maa (Teevra), Paa, Nee(Shuddh), Saa	**Shree**	Saa, Re (Komal), Maa (Teevra), Paa, Nee (Shuddh), Saa
Maalkauns	Saa, Gaa (Komal), Maa, Dhaa (Komal), Nee (Komal) Saa	**Maalkauns**	Saa, Gaa (Komal), Maa, Dhaa (Komal), Nee (Komal), Saa
Hindol	Saa, Gaa, Maa (Teevra), Dha, Nee, Saa	**Hindol**	Saa, Gaa, Maa (Teevra), Dha, Nee, Saa
Bhairav	Saa, Re (Komal), Gaa, Maa, Paa, Dhaa (Komal), Nee, Saa	**Bhairav**	Saa, Re (Komal), Gaa, Maa, Paa, Dhaa (Komal) Nee, Saa
Nat	Saa, Re, Gaa, Maa, Paa, Dhaa, Nee, Saa	**Deepak**	Saa, Re, Gaa, Maa (Teevra), Paa Dhaa, Nee, Saa

By this arrangement, we have two ragas with the notes Saa, Re, Maa, Paa, Nee, Saa, two with Saa, Gaa, Maa, Dhaa, Nee, Saa and two with Saa, Re, Gaa, Maa, Paa, Dha, Nee, Saa (four ragas being odav and two sampoorna). In the first two you have Saa, Ree, Maa, Paa, Nee, Saa. This scale, with Nee Komal, is Megh. With the Re, Maa and Nee reversed of Megh you get Shree (as Saa and Paa are unchangeable or achal swaras). In the next set you have Saa, Gaa, Maa, Dhaa, Nee, Saa, which is Maalkauns. Maa, Dhaa and Nee again reversed (of Maalkauns) give you Hindol—Saa, Gaa, Maa, Dhaa, Nee, Saa. Then comes the third category, Saa, Re, Gaa, Maa, Paa, Dhaa, Nee, Saa. This is Bhairav. Now the controversy is: either Nat or Deepak. Those who believe in Nat, change only the Re and Dha of Bhairav, and not its Maa; they come to Nat as a result. Those who change the three notes, Re, Maa and Dhaa, come to Eman. I have heard from Shri S.N. Ratanjankar that there was the possibility of Deepak being from Poorvee thaath; he also believed that today's Eman could have been Deepak at one time. Deepak from Poorvee thaath is nothing but the addition of one Teevra Madhyam in Bhairav, as the addition of a note is not a policy in the pattern of the six ragas throughout. One more argument for Deepak being today's Eman or Kalyaan is the similarity of the time prescribed for their singing. Only a raga sung in the evening can bear the name of Deepak (and Eman is one of the most popular of the evening melodies). So Deepak vanished—not as a melody but as a name.

Gandhaar graam has vanished into heaven

One of the myths that have come down to us is that the 'gandhaar graam has been lost' to heaven, or as they say, *lop ho gayaa* (lop meaning lost). What does this mean?

Graam means 'township'. There were three graams mentioned in our ancient texts—shadaj graam, madhyam graam and gandhaar graam. Planning of the graam is based on samvaad (harmony); so there can be three sets of notes in the scale based on samvaad (harmony); shadaj madhyam samvaad, shadaj-pancham samvaad and the shadaj-gandhaar relation.

The harmonic relationship between the third and fifth notes (Gaa+Paa) has been universally accepted everywhere. Now let us study the Saa-Paa township or graam, that is, shadaj graam or Saa-Paa samvaad. We are measuring the relationship of each note to its fifth note.

Saa to Paa
Paa to Re (Shuddh)
Re (Shuddh) to Dhaa (Shuddh)
Dhaa (Shuddh) to Gaa (Shuddh)
Gaa (Shuddh) to Nee (Shuddh)
Nee to Maa (Teevra)
Maa (Teevra) to Re (Komal)
Re (Komal) to Dhaa (Komal)
Dhaa (Komal) to Gaa (Komal)
Gaa (Komal) to Nee (Komal)
Nee (Komal) to Maa (Shuddh)
Maa (Shuddh) to Saa

Coming back to Saa, we complete the township. Thus, improvising on the Saa-Paa relationship and covering all the twelve notes is shadaj graam. Saa-Paa is in other words, Paa-Saa also, now covering the Paa-Saa relationship, in other words Saa-Maa (distance-wise). Improvising the Saa-Maa relationship and covering twelve notes is madhyam graam. This is elaborated below:

Saa to Maa
Maa to Nee (Komal)

Nee (Komal) to Gaa (Komal)
Gaa (Komal) to Dhaa (Komal)
Dhaa (Komal) to Re (Komal)
Re (Komal) to Maa (Teevra)
Maa (Teevra) to Nee (Shuddh)
Nee (Shuddh) to Gaa (Shuddh)
Gaa (Shuddh) to Dhaa (Shuddh)
Dhaa (Shuddh) to Re (Shuddh)
Re (Shuddh) to Paa
Paa to Saa

Now about the gandhaar graam, which is supposed to be lost in heaven. The improvisation of the relationship of third note from Saa, that is, Gaa, is:

Saa to Gaa (Shuddh)
Gaa (Shuddh) to Dhaa (Komal)
Dhaa (Komal) to Saa

That means, only three notes are covered in this graam. That is why it is considered 'lost'. Not completing the twelve notes, this third-note relationship is lost in the very third combination, and the third combination merges into Saa. So although the third relationship is natural, you cannot see the other notes through this samvaad.

In other words, to put it in very simple terms, in the township of twelve notes we have three possible angles to see the whole township through: from Saa we see twelve notes (that is called Saa-Paa samvaad or shadaj graam); in the gandhaar graam we see only three notes out of twelve, which is why it is said that this graam is lost (to the heavens).

The naming of lesser-known ragas

When we look into the logic of the naming of ragas today, and at the working out of raga compounds and raga evolution, we find that unfortunately the subject has given rise to much dispute among practitioners of different gharaanaas. It is natural of course to have controversies about lesser-known ragas. I have not dealt with ragas in this dictionary for reasons explained already in the Introduction, but would like to say a few words about the naming of lesser-known ragas.

In the past, raga controversies arose perhaps because of the lack of written records (notation, etc). There are many ragas, with the same notes and structure that have different names in different gharaanaas. Musically, they bear no differences or have the most negligible difference. For example, every musician will agree that there is practically no difference between Aasaavaree of Shuddh Re and Jaunpuree. Raga Pancham is known as Aadee Basant in one school and Maarwa Thaath kee Lalit in another. Apart from this, V.N. Patwardhan in *Raga Vigyaan* mentions this Lalit as lalitaavaree.

Now all these names are justified, due to some reason or the other. For if we proceed in terms of moorchhana from the Pancham of Aadee Basant (popular), it is known as Aadee Basant. Hence the names Pancham and Aadee Basant are understandable. Maarwa Thaath kee Lalit is also incorrect, as in the overall structure Lalit with Shuddh Dhaa becomes Maarwaa Thaath kee Lalit.

Now take Pancham Kalyaan. There are some very interesting recent versions of this raga. Taking Pancham as the basic note of the raga Pooriyaa Kalyaan, we proceed in terms of moorchhana. The late Pannalal Ghosh, well-known flautist, had intoduced this raga as Deepaavalee. However, I renamed it as Pancham Kalyaan because it definitely ends up in the Kalyaan group of ragas. The

Pancham of Pooriyaa Kalyaan was a significant factor in coming to this decision.

I take this opportunity to dwell on a few examples of ragas that have struck my mind over these years, illustrating the manner in which new ragas take shape and are named. Take the instance of Gunkalee's Madhyam. Proceeding from this note in terms of moorchhana we will get Maa Paa Dhaa Saa Re Maa. As Saa Re Gaa Paa Dhaa Saa (which is now the new scale) belongs to the Ranjanee group of ragas, this scale should be known as Gunranjanee. Similarly, take Maaru Basant. It is Maru in the first half and Basant in the second. Or, Shaam-Bhoop: it is Shaam in aarohee and Bhoop in avrohee. Introducing Shuddh Dhaa in Gunkalee (Shuddh in aarohee and Komal in avrohee) we get a very beautiful melody, which I named Amarkalee.

Groups of ragas with a common pakar (haunt) are thought out for the naming of ragas. For example, Gaa Maa Re Saa (Ga Komal) can easily be thought out in the Kanhada group, Re Gaa Re Saa (Ree Gaa Komal) can bear the name of the Todee group and Maa Re Paa can be fixed for any Malhaar and so on.

Thus, the great need of the hour is a common platform where representatives of different gharaanaas can come together, standardize raga names, and give a new coherence to the fast-evolving grammar of our music.

Acknowledgements

The long-cherished dream of wanting to share this book of Guruji with everyone is coming true, for which I have one and only Shantanu Ray Chaudhuri to thank. For his faith in me in writing the foreword, eternal patience waiting for me to submit the draft and then editing and giving it shape! Thanks also to Afeefa Baig for her work on the book.

Gajra, my Guru Behan, for supporting me and encouraging me.

Nisha Mahajan, for the updates on artiste profiles with additional text and further confirming details with Manjari Sinha.

Devansh Aggarwal, for reading so many drafts and giving his fair opinion as a young reader.

Aasmaan Bhardwaj and Vishal, for reading the first draft and giving me the courage to complete it.

Taiyeb Badr, for his immediate reaction and insight on the foreword!

Rekha Bhardwaj